How to Get the Upper Hand

How to Get the

Upper Hand

RALPH CHARELL

STEIN AND DAY/*Publishers*/New York

First published in 1978
THIRD PRINTING, 1978
Copyright © 1978 by Ralph Charell
All rights reserved
Designed by Ed Kaplin
Printed in the United States of America
Stein and Day/*Publishers*/Scarborough House,
Briarcliff Manor, N.Y. 10510

Library of Congress Cataloging in Publication Data
Charell, Ralph.
   How to get the upper hand.

   1. Negotiation.   2. Success.   I. Title.
BF637.N4C45   158'.1   77-8761
ISBN 0-8128-2336-2

He who does not have a dog to hunt with—
must use a cat.

Brazilian proverb

Contents

CONTENTS

How to Get the Upper Hand

1 Opening

In a previous work, *How I Turn Ordinary Complaints into Thousands of Dollars: The Diary of a Tough Customer,* I demonstrated that properly handled consumer complaints were items of value. They could be viewed not merely as problems but also as opportunities readily convertible to cash. Using actual names, dates, and places, I described a number of encounters with giant corporations, conglomerates, department stores, public utilities, professionals, bureaucrats, and others, in which I employed methods and techniques of my own devising, to cope with bad goods and terrible services and the indifference, incompetence, deceit, and pro-

13

crastination that often accompany them. At the time the book was published, I had exchanged my own justified consumer complaints for a sum in excess of $75,000 and *The Guinness Book of World Records* recognized me as "the world's most successful complainer."

In publicizing the book, I visited approximately 30 cities and was interviewed hundreds of times on television, radio, and in the press. I also had the opportunity to speak directly with scores of people on telephone call-in programs, and many others corresponded. I heard and read lots of complaints about automobiles and appliances that broke down; undelivered mail order products; overpriced, uncaring professionals; delivery and repair people who never arrived; and the like, but it soon became apparent that many of the complaints were much more fundamental.

I had a growing sense of great and widespread distress. People's lives had not worked out as they'd hoped and dreamed. The events that affected their lives had gotten too big and too complicated for their own efforts to determine the outcome. Life had become a series of unwelcome surprises, of collisions, in which people were always at the mercy of circumstances beyond their control. They were being worn down daily. The present was joyless, a painful struggle, and opportunities lay only in the future or the past.

Many were convinced nobody out there cared about their individual welfare, that they were being manipulated to benefit an interest other than their own. They were becoming distrustful, isolated, cynical, desensitized, and deadened. Some thought socially disapproved behavior was required to achieve many of their goals. I recognized the feelings they were describing for I had worked my way through the same terrain several years earlier.

At first, I responded by trying to provide practical suggestions for dealing with each of the specific consumer complaints described to me. But it became increasingly difficult to ignore the more significant problems. As a lay person, I was not sure I could be of help despite my best intentions. I began to adapt some of the methods and techniques I'd used successfully in consumer-complaint situations to "complaints about life" situations. The results encouraged me to develop additional methods and techniques for mastering many of the basic problems of daily living we all face. As I'd done with consumer complaints, I also began to devise means for preventing the problems from arising in the first place.

Creating and using the various means of getting the upper hand set forth in these pages has been a joyful, liberating experience. I pass them along not only for the pleasure and surcease they will provide but also in the hope their widespread use will produce a ripple effect that will finally brake the conduct they are designed to control.

2 On to Shangri-La

We all spend too much of our lives running through mazes others put before us. We are so intent on learning each new maze we don't stop to think that the best route may be around, not through, the maze. Or over or under or away from, or not at all. The underlying idea of *How to Get the Upper Hand* is that we can always create room in which to maneuver, no matter how cramped our lives, if we accept the fact that we are not automatons.

As human beings, we have choices to exercise, no matter how tiny or seemingly insignificant. And by exercising this or that choice, in one way or another, in one sequence or another, we can exert a force, no matter how slight. If we permit ourselves to grapple with a particular reality in our life, we can add our own weight and imagination and momentum to the situation, no matter what it is, and thereby affect it. We are not inert, lifeless matter that must necessarily be the recipient of a set of givens over which we have nothing to say or do except what is programmed for us. Our responses need not be automatic and passive. We can truly cause certain things to happen by employing simple methods and techniques anybody can learn. We can act upon our environment, not simply react to it. And when we have taken charge of a particular situation and altered it to our liking, the good feelings that result are ours as a bonus.

Sometimes, in one beautifully easy move, we will be able to turn the tumblers of a given lock so the door swings open to our slightest touch. At other times the route may be less direct. We may have to keep adding values to our side more slowly until the cumulative weight and pressure are irresistible. Still other times we may have to create a momentum out of sheer will or nerve until all obstacles are overwhelmed before its dynamic energy. Occasionally we may have to tunnel our way under or around, or create a bridge that spans the distance between where we are and our objective.

Regardless of the winning method we use, our efforts will become more and more skillful, better focused and coordinated, and more readily effective, with practice. As a starting point, I have set forth a number of methods and techniques for dealing with typically nettlesome people, places, and things. All of the examples are simple and practical. They will work for you as they've worked for me and others, and you will feel good, as I have, when they do.

Once you begin to get the feel of this new approach, my hope is you will begin to develop your own methods and techniques for dealing with any other situations you wish to alter or control. As in the process of addition, once you learn the method, *all* sums can be found. So, too, in getting the upper hand and taking charge of your own life—once you have determined you can and should do so and have learned some of the basic principles—the path to your own private version of Shangri-La will be nearer at hand.

3 How to Stop Doctors from Keeping You Waiting

Let's say we fell ill enough to call a doctor. We'd like to see him (or her) at one o'clock but the only appointment we can get is at eleven. When we arrive at eleven, we will typically find that six or seven other people were also given eleven o'clock appointments so we'll have to sit in the waiting room for an indeterminate period, surrounded by other ill people, some of whom probably have communicable diseases. Finally, at about one o'clock (the original time we'd requested), after we have waited two hours, our name is called.

It's difficult to deal with this situation, yet it's clearly unacceptable. What element can we introduce to alter it to our liking? How can we get the upper hand?

For years, I seethed but accepted this treatment. After much thought, I came up with a new approach. Sometimes, I'm able to obtain an immediate preference by courteously and quietly (but in a businesslike manner) telling the receptionist that I had an appointment at eleven, it's now ten after eleven, and I would appreciate the earliest opportunity to see the doctor as I have a pressing schedule which has been further jammed by the inconvenient scheduling of the appointment. And I'm also not feeling too well. A smile is helpful in this connection and one should show no trace of irascibility. This approach is not infallible.

If I actually have to spend an hour and a half, or two, sitting there, I wheel into action when I get the doctor's bill. I'm in good health by then and on my own turf. Suppose, for example, he bills me $35 for the visit. Well, right on his bill, I bill him for two hours of waiting time, at a nominal $25 per hour, a total of $50 dollars. Then I give him a $15 professional discount. When I substract my $35 bill from his, the balance due is zero.

I don't do this because I want, or expect, payment from the doctor. But when the doctor's receptionist or secretary gets my bill canceling the doctor's bill, I'm going to get a telephone call. I will then explain that my time is either more valuable than the doctor's, equally valuable, or less valuable, but that it clearly has a value and that value should be respected. I will then express my willingness to make an exception in this case and pay the doctor's bill, but only on the understanding that the next time I make an appointment and I arrive on time, I expect to see the doctor at once, barring some real and rare emergency. And the beautiful payoff is that the next time I arrive, I find the same roomful of waiting patients, but after a short wait the receptionist calls my name and I walk right in smiling benignly.

4 How to Bypass a Computer and Reach a Human Being

One of the problems we all face is trying to correct an erroneous computerized bill. I've learned from experience that calling, writing, pleading, and threatening is usually a waste of time. The computer keeps repeating the error, as it's programmed to, and then, sometimes, it has the effrontery to tell other computers my credit is no longer as good as it was. How's this for a way to break this pattern?

As I've learned to anticipate that my efforts are probably going to be ignored, I now use a different approach. I simply take a pencil or a pen and punch out two or three of the computer punch card marks. It can actually feel good to do this. I then write a message on the card in basic English, explaining the error and how to correct it, and send the card back.

The computer can no longer process my card. When the machine rejects it, a person, a human being, will see the rejected card and be able to read my message telling whoever finds the card how to correct the error. As it's much more expensive to handle computer punch cards individually and personally than mechanically in large batches, I've given the company a good, pocketbook reason to correct its error, and this method, therefore, usually works the first time.

However, if the error is repeated, the next time I get the company's computer punch card, I do exactly the same thing again, except that at the top of the card, in big letters, I write "FINAL NOTICE."

5 How to Apply the Brakes to Telephone Time Wasters

Who can resist a ringing telephone? Even tormented, desperate characters without a single hope left and bent on self-destruction have been lured from narrow ledges by the seductive promise of its rhythmic insistence. How many times have you and I succumbed to its peals after we'd stepped into the shower or at the moment we sat down to enjoy a good dinner, or at other inopportune times, to our mounting regret? The telephone, a live-in Trojan horse we all possess, exacts additional tribute beyond its accustomed monthly tolls.

You no sooner hold the receiver to your ear than you realize, with a twinge, you are going to be suspended in the timeless quicksand of an interminable talker. You've been selected by a friend, relative, or business associate, for the depositing of a mountain of problems in glittering detail on your shoulders. Your head has begun to throb from the un-relieved unburdening and your throat has gone dry from just listening, but there is no abatement. You're too civilized to hang up abruptly; you wish the instrument would suddenly malfunction, but it only does so when you most want to converse. Why be at the beck and call of any-one who has a dime? How can you break free of this bind?

I use and recommend an audio cassette on which I've prerecorded the sound of a ringing telephone. I keep it handy. Whenever I wish, I simply insert the cassette and press the start button. I keep the cassette player near enough to the telephone I'm trying to get off so it can be heard clearly and distinctly by the party I want to avoid.

If, after a couple of rings, the other party doesn't ask whether I'd like to take the other call (a lack of civility not uncommon in these cases), I excuse myself and stop the cassette player. After a significant pause that establishes the other call, I come back on the line and say that I'm terribly sorry but I've got to go.

Often, this will restore a sense of propriety to the caller and he or she will realize the call has been over extended. But whether or not this occurs, I'm off the hook without bruising any egos. And for those who don't have a second telephone, I recommend the sound of a doorbell. Where there's a will there's a way!

6 How to Get Red-Carpet Treatment

In January 1974 Charles Osgood interviewed me on the CBS Morning News. It was the beginning of the publicity tour on a book I'd written. Mr. Osgood displayed his characteristic good humor and charm and the segment went very well. I was feeling pretty good as the publisher's publicity director and I prepared to leave the studio for breakfast. As we were going out the door, I was told that a woman in Georgia was on the line and had asked to speak with me. I said I'd be happy to take the long-distance call.

The woman told me she had been a patient in a Georgia hospital where she'd been referred with a kidney ailment.

After some cursory tests she'd been discharged. No treatment of any kind had been prescribed but she still had the kidney ailment and felt weak and ill. She asked whether I could advise her how to get needed hospital attention, and she sounded extremely upset and unhappy. At first, I didn't know how to respond. I realized I didn't have many of the facts, but the woman sounded so distraught and forlorn I wanted to try to come up with something by way of helping, even if it were not too well thought out.

"What's the name of the governor of Georgia?" I asked, after thinking for a few moments.

"Carter. Jimmy Carter."

"Hm. Carter's too common a name," I said. "Let's try Senator Stennis of Mississippi. You might consider this: Check into another hospital in Georgia but this time use the name Stennis as your middle name, as if it's your family name. I don't think the senator will mind. Everybody will know that name. And when they ask you whether you're related to Senator Stennis, just say you don't want *any* special treatment because of your family connections."

There isn't much doubt that if the woman acted upon that suggestion (and she loved the idea and seemed to brighten immediately) she received red-carpet treatment. While it may be unfortunate to use a stratagem like that, I thought it even more unfortunate that a person with the nation's fourth-largest killer disease had been given such short shrift at the first hospital.

I've often thought about that incident. We all know that some people go through life with certain names that seem to unfurl red carpets magically for them wherever they go while the rest of us are given tangled weeds and shifting sands to tread, or we're faced with high electrified fences patrolled by underfed guard dogs. What a marvelous bonus it would be for us if *we* could receive the special courtesies and myriad deferences that regularly smooth the way for a favored few.

Wealth, power, and glamour account for a good many of the niceties so unstintingly bestowed. We may not be able to attain these attributes instantly. But we can instantly apply a new label that commands preferred status; for these special favors are not confined to the particular personage with the honored name. The entire family shares the benefits. Are we to be denied civility merely because our names are unfamiliar and contain no Roman numeral suffixes, titles of royalty or nobility, or hyphens? Should mere nomenclature needlessly deprive us of a full share of common courtesy from those we favor with our trade? By no means.

If the use of Senator Stennis's name could obtain superior medical care for the woman in Georgia, imagine how we can innocently extend this technique to make our dealings more pleasant. And in employing this technique are we not also creating pleasure for others as well as ourselves, for if appearances are reliable, merchants, tradespeople, and service personnel seem to derive special joys from larding numberless attentions on the Very Important Persons they vie to attend, while the less distinguished bleat themselves hoarse or are forced to fend for themselves.

In practice, name dropping has scores of applications. Let's say, for example, you're planning a vacation. It's not difficult to find out before you leave who Mr. Big is at the hotel, the airline, the steamship company, or whatever, with which you will be dealing. This may be done by asking a stockbroker or your local librarian for the name of the person in charge. The president and board chairperson, or the owner or managing director, depending upon local custom, will do nicely. The loftier the title and the more physically remote from where you will be, the better. Then, each time you make a reservation or ask for your telephone messages or check in, use the last name of Mr. Big as your middle name or even your first name. Special treatment will be accorded you wherever you go, and you may soon begin to expect these privileges as a new confidence and serenity heal past wounds.

One more suggestion: Other things being equal, if you have a choice between dealing with a company that is operating profitably and one losing money, choose the former. Nothing chills good instincts and notions of fair play and stoppers ears to reason as quickly as red ink on the income statement. And it doesn't take long for this kind of bottom line thinking at the top to percolate right down to the ground floor of the corporation. On the other hand, profits are associated with good management, and the latter tend to deal more forthrightly with their customers, for inculcating and maintaining customer good will and dealing fairly with the public is part of good management.

If your choice includes more than one profitable company, I'd tend to choose the one whose earnings have shown the greatest percentage improvement in the past quarter. Euphoria is communicable as well as panic. A stock broker or your local librarian can supply these figures readily. Of course, if there's a significant price differential or irresistible extras in one of the choices, this must be factored into your decision. But often the product or service and the price and terms are identical or substantially indistinguishable, and in these cases we may be able to choose the company more likely to please us instead of the company which has implemented a dreary cost-cutting policy. And if, perchance, something goes awry, we are more likely to be ultimately satisfied by the profitable company. This approach would seem to be another way of making it easy for the other side of the transaction to please us.

7 How to Reach the Always Unavailable Mr. Big

Mr. Big (or Ms. Big) is the person in charge of a particular area in which we're having a problem—the corporate executive of a large company who has the authority and the competence quickly to put things right for us. But he (or she) is never in when we call, and our calls are never returned. The closest we are ordinarily allowed to get to Mr. Big is to miss him narrowly or to find him in his office but "in conference" and therefore incommunicado, or out to us.

We are not always this lucky, for his meetings are sometimes on another floor, out of the building or the city, or even abroad. Our calls to Mr. Big are continually shuttled and shuffled from underling to underling while our days turn to nights, our minds to jelly. We may find people who wish to be helpful but don't understand, or who lack jurisdiction to handle matters involving more than the cost of a soft drink.

Only Mr. Big has the happy combination of intelligence and the authority to help us, but he is never available. Our letters to him, if we take the time to write, are unanswered, or are passed to others who may finally direct a vague and unsatisfactory form letter to us with a great show of concern and professions of earnestness. But there is no sign of Mr. Big except, possibly, a reference in the form letter to his passing along our letter to the undersigned for response. How then can we cause Mr. Big to speak with us and motivate him to resolve our problem?

My approach is to call Mr. Big person-to-person, which can even be done locally by dialing the numeral zero (operator) followed by the telephone number. For a slight additional charge (but only if we reach our party) we enlist the services of a telephone company operator who sounds at least semiofficial, an improvement over our wonted overconciliatory murmur. It adds stature to the call and takes it out of the usual pattern, helping to create a better effect. More often than not, it's also free, as opposed to the wasted money spent in the past pursuing the elusive Mr. Big.

When the operator tells whoever picks up Mr. Big's telephone that Mr. Charell is calling Mr. Big, the secretary or assistant will typically reply that Mr. Big is in Istanbul or wherever. At that precise moment I come into the conversation and deliver the line I've been rehearsing:

"This is a matter Mr. Big can handle rather easily but if he's unavailable, would you kindly transfer this call to Mr. Bigger?"

I then instruct the operator, after a pause during which the assistant, the operator, and I are still telephonically connected, to make this call person-to-person to Mr. Bigger. I have, of course, gotten Mr. Bigger's name from the same place I got Mr. Big's—by asking the switchboard operator the name of the person in charge of the area that concerns me and to whom that individual reports—or by checking the names of top management with a stockbroker or librarian.

Mr. Big's assistant or secretary has now been given a decision to make that requires speedy handling. He or she knows that people in high corporate places, like his or her boss, don't like waves made in their direction. The last thing Mr. Big wants is for his boss to be disturbed by a routine matter Mr. Big tried to evade.

If Mr. Big is actually in his office, perhaps doing the crossword puzzle with his feet up on the desk, or struggling with the big decision of the morning like where and with whom to have lunch, there will probably be a lengthening pause, a hurried exchange, and I will be told that Mr. Big has just returned to his office: "He's just rounding the corridor now, Mr. Charell." He didn't drop out of the skies from Istanbul?

If he is actually unavailable at the moment, the secretary or assistant, reluctant to transfer the call to Mr. Bigger, will assure me that Mr. Big will get right back to me. I usually put a time limit on the return call by stating that I will be at my office only until some specific time and getting the secretary's assurance that Mr. Big will return the call before I leave. Whether Mr. Big returns the call or takes it at once, his attention and courtesy are exemplary, for he's been given some personal motivation. He knows that unless I'm pleased with his handling of the matter I set

33

before him, there's an excellent chance Mr. Bigger will hear about it. This introduces an element of jeopardy for Mr. Big because of his chronic unavailability, about which I comment to him, plus his poor handling of a good customer's problem. He also knows that any help he gives me, even if it's somewhat beyond the norm, is being paid for by somebody else, usually the stockholders.

8 How to Find Room at the Inn

I've enjoyed staying at hotels all over the country. Spacious, quiet, well-situated accommodations, superior food, a wide assortment of prompt, courteous services, and all the other amenities and conveniences of a first-rate hotel are particularly appreciated.Sometimes, however, the best hotels may cost a bit more than we wish to pay and we may decide to settle for less than the best. Problems are almost certain to arise.

One of the most difficult to cope with is overbooking. We arrive, weary and hungry, with our reservation, but we're turned away into the night. It's heartening, therefore, to report how one man solved this problem by causing the right effect.

Our man arrived at a hotel late one night and began to register. The room clerk peered at his name as he was writing it, squinting to read the inverted block letters, and asked whether he had a reservation. The traveler replied that he did. After some futile looking for the guest's reservation, the clerk asked whether his reservation had been confirmed. It hadn't.

Whereupon the traveler was informed there was no reservation for him to be found and no rooms were available. The remonstrances and slight indignation of our man failed to impress the clerk, who was becoming visibly bored. Without a *confirmed* reservation there was simply no way the would-be guest could stay at that hotel and that was that. Period. Another innocent was to be stranded far from home, hungry and tired. But our man knew how to get the upper hand!

Overbooking was bad enough in his view. But when the overbooker was also overbearing, it was time to take a stand. Our man told the unfeeling room clerk that to him a reservation was a reservation. And that, therefore, if his room were not yet ready, he would simply get undressed and retire right there in the lobby.

No sooner had he removed his jacket and unbuckled his belt than the inhospitable hotel man folded the hand. In a twinkling, the traveler was registered and was last seen being followed into an elevator by a solicitous bellman.

9 "Gaslighting": The Art of Disorienting Your Antagonist

So far, we have seen a few examples of how to get the upper hand, how to make certain things happen that produce desired results. The audio tape cassette created the illusion of a ringing telephone and allowed the caller who was imposing on our time and good will to become aware of other conflicting demands on our time. In the case of the erroneous computerized bill, we provided a means of bringing the error to the attention of somebody who could correct it, facilitated the correction by supplying the solution, and made it expensive to ignore. By billing the doctor who kept us waiting, we dramatically established in the mind of the doctor's receptionist that our time, too, was valuable. We reached Mr. Big by introducing the concept of possible personal jeopardy for him and the idea that he was not the supreme authority in dealing with us. In the hotel situation, the stakes were suddenly raised to the point where the room clerk couldn't risk calling the bet.

Illusion, economic motivation, an unusual way of making a point, jeopardy, and a sudden raising of the stakes have been the principal means we have so far employed to cause effects. In all of these situations, the results were not long in coming. Sometimes, however, an effect must be built more slowly, as in the technique of "gaslighting." I've never personally swung this iron, but if you'd like to play with a full set of clubs in the bag, this technique should be described. Even if we don't use it, there is value in being aware of it so that we may be better able to defend against it, if necessary. In that spirit, I pass along the following example.

Retail clerks are able to put us off out of all proportion to their apparent resources. By becoming engaged by somebody else when, at long last, it is our turn; by gossiping with co-workers in small clusters, while we try in vain to hail them; by endless dawdling; and in a number of other small but telling ways, they are able to induce tics in otherwise poised and stable freeholders.

If we create a scene, we are contemptible. If we complain to a supervisor, where is our proof? And we are certain to be thought odd, for a description of what happened requires a subtlety of articulation on our part and a receptivity and understanding on the part of the listener rarely found even among philosophers discoursing with one another. We may also expect steadfast denial among the co-workers. And there is never enough time. Where, then, lies our remedy? Perhaps in "gaslighting."

In the play *Gaslight*, by Patrick Hamilton (which came to Broadway in 1941 as *Angel Street*, and was adapted into a film starring Ingrid Bergman and Charles Boyer under the original English title), Mr. Manningham attempts to drive his wife mad slowly by managing and controlling events so as to cause her to question her own sanity. He would, for example, deliberately hide ordinary household objects and accuse her of their senseless, mindless theft. When the objects were later found among her belongings where he'd put them or, more damaging, when she could lead him to one of the missing articles (not because she'd misappropriated it but only because she knew it had been found there twice before), her mental faculties were called into serious question, even by herself.

This disorientation of the antagonist can be useful in certain cases. While its purpose may sometimes appear merely retaliatory, "gaslighting" can also help rehabilitate an otherwise incorrigible antagonist. And it can help us get the upper hand by drawing the attention of somebody in a position to muzzle the behavior we find undesirable.

In response to a post card announcing a shoe sale, a "gaslighting" enthusiast journeyed to a midtown Manhattan department store. He spent some time in the crush of the small, crowded shoe boutique, only to be told the shoes he wished to try on were not part of the sale. His salesperson soon left the immediate area, ostensibly to procure some more shoes. After much additional time had elapsed the ill-used customer learned, on inquiry, that the man had gone to lunch and left him sitting there unattended, with one shoe on and one off.

The angry "gaslighter" decided to put some of his knowledge to practical use. At a nearby dramatic school, he soon located a student who, like himself, was middle-aged, tall, and husky but whose feet were almost two sizes smaller. A brief conversation and a surprisingly small fee were all it took to hire the actor's services for he, too, was eager to put his studies to practical use. The wardrobe and makeup departments of the drama school were small but serviceable and the plan began to mature.

The drama student arrived at the store and arranged to be waited on by the offending clerk, who had by that time returned from lunch. A punctilious man with a Vandyke beard and pince-nez, in a black suit with a watchchain across his vest and carrying a walking stick, the drama student, playing to the nonexistent gallery in his mind, was soon able to exasperate the clerk to the edge of his patience by insisting on several careful measurements of both of his feet in order to ensure a perfect fit.

When the clerk returned with a couple of pairs of shoes, the drama student (despite the fact that the shoes fit perfectly) insisted on a smaller size, as prearranged. As the clerk, balancing neatly between outburst and indigestion, left for more shoes, the drama student (taking mental curtain calls) left the boutique, tossing the walking stick, with a wink, to the identically turned out "gaslighter," who took his place.

The rest went exactly as planned: the vain jamming of his foot into each successive left shoe before the startled eyes of the clerk; the instant replay for the irately summoned manager; the astonished silence, in lieu of an explanation, from the clerk; the stalking out of the shop

40

with the promise to do no further business with the company and to contact those in charge; and the continuing puzzled consternation of another ill-natured salesman. Had he chosen to remain on the scene, our friend would no doubt have received special treatment; but rehabilitation, not mere shoe selection, was his objective.

10 How Your Dog May Fly with You Instead of the Cargo

 A New York actor, whose career had been less than spectacular, finally got a break. A series had been sold to one of the television networks based upon a pilot in which he'd been featured, and the producer wanted him to continue in the role. Very good bucks and a chance for steady work at last! The actor and his wife were overjoyed.

They threw a farewell party for themselves, sold or gave away most of their furniture, shipped the rest to their rented house in Beverly Hills, and began to anticipate the great new life they were going to enjoy on the sunny coast. They even considered the possibility of having a child. Up to that point, the only other member of their immediate family was a four-and-a-half year-old Weimaraner that they'd raised since he was a pup.

Wimpy was a beautiful animal. The original reason, or more accurately, pretext, for buying him was that he'd make a good watchdog if an out of town job caused the actor to leave his wife alone for a few days in their West Side apartment. But the real reason Wimpy had been adopted was that he was pretty and gentle and playful, and they loved him. He was still as gentle and playful as the day they brought him home, although he now weighed 46 pounds and had a set of teeth that could tear through a telephone book. The Weimaraner loved the couple and would actually have been an excellent watchdog but he'd never been put to the test, for the only out of town job the actor had been offered since Wimpy moved in was a season of stock and they'd all spent that summer together.

Now they were all leaving town together again. But this time Wimpy wouldn't be able to stretch out in the back seat of a rented car. All the airlines had been polite and patient, but firm: only pets small enough to fit into a carrying case to be placed under the seat would be boarded in the cabin with passengers. Because Wimpy was too large for this, the actor and his wife would have to buy a collapsible carrier (36x24x27 inches) and pen Wimpy inside it! The poor caged guy would be placed on a conveyor belt, like luggage, to disappear from their sight, scared and alone, consigned to the belly of the aircraft with the cargo.

The actor and his wife called the airlines repeatedly, sometimes on two extensions of the same line, seeking in vain any nuance in the rules which would permit Wimpy to ride with them. But the airlines said it was not possible, even if they bought him a first class ticket. One reservations

43

clerk assured them that the temperature in the baggage compartment was maintained at fifty to seventy degrees. Fifty was cold enough but friends reported cases of dogs that had practically frozen solid on long flights. And they heard of animals left out on ramps alone for hours after the plane landed. Sometimes pets were lost. Maybe baggage would fall on his little makeshift kennel. They were told of one incident in which a flight attendant gave a frightened dog a tranquilizer meant for an adult, and the animal had to be rushed to a hospital, which barely saved the dog's life. One airline said it minimized the carbon dioxide in the baggage compartment by limiting the number of animals in each section. Carbon dioxide! Minimized? That didn't sound too good. Not for Wimpy.

They began to examine other possibilities, but there were no easy answers. A coast to coast train trip would take several days and the dog would be cramped and without exercise. They heard about a bus ticket that would allow them to get on and off at will, but that voyage would take more than a fortnight if they had to keep stopping with the dog. And where would they spend all those nights? And the cost would have been punishing even if they had the time, which they didn't. The contract called for the actor to report on the set in six days and he was already reading scripts. A rented car posed similar problems. What to do?

As the departure date drew nearer, the couple's delight with their improved prospects was considerably diluted with apprehension about Wimpy. If only some benevolent spirit could wave a wand that would permit Wimpy to board with them. How would this harm anybody? He'd already been such a good sport about taking his rabies shot as required by the State of California. They refused to accept Wimpy's fate. The little guy depended on them and they would never betray his trust. They continued to think about the problem long hours into the night.

It was a bright, sunny spring morning as Wimpy and his owners approached Kennedy Airport by taxi. A porter outside the terminal took care of the bags. The couple sat quietly in the lounge as they waited for their flight to be called.

About five minutes before boarding time, a man about the same height and weight as the actor was escorted toward the boarding ramp by an airline employee. But for the beard and the dark glasses and the white cane, the man might easily have been taken for the actor. He was also accompanied by a gray Seeing-Eye dog in harness.

A few minutes later, the other passengers boarded. The big dog thumped his tail against the cabin floor in joyful recognition as a woman slid into the seat beside the man with the cane.

11 Keeping the Lid On

Visitors from abroad often remark on the strange sight of steam billowing from below ground level on the streets of New York. Sophisticated cosmopolitans (who no longer remember their own initial surprise) nonchalantly explain the phenomenon as merely a "Con Ed steam hole." Con Ed (easily mistaken for the nickname of someone familiar with the insides of prisons) is, of course, the much advertised and publicized name of the gas and electric company whose rates are the highest in the country.

Long after visitors have become accustomed to these "First Circle" effects, the natives must still writhe and twitch with Con Edification even more infernal. The reference is to Con Ed's ill-fitting manhole covers, ubiquitous as mid-December Santas, which clang and clatter continually, adding to the sleeplessness and irritability of a population already half-crazed by overcrowding.

When a vehicle passes over the rim of a loose manhole cover, the initial effect is that its weight depresses one sector of the cover, with a clank, and raises another sector. When the weight of the vehicle suddenly leaves the rim of the cover, the raised portion is permitted to fall back with a loud metallic clang. This incessant clank/clang is played out throughout the city 24 hours a day.

During daylight hours, this unnecessary noise is submerged in the irregular cacophony of a busy, traffic-snarled, crowded city in a frenzy of perpetual construction and demolition. But as night falls and those who haven't deserted the city for outlying bedrooms prepare for the blessed, merciful repairs of a night's sleep, clank and his bullying big brother, clang, come into their own.

My bedroom overlooks a major crosstown artery of traffic, which gives clang hundreds of opportunities to disturb even my deepest slumbers. No respecter of person or distance (I live more than 100 feet above the street), clang insists on being heard again and again. And clang has more relatives than the Kallikaks, all cast from the same antisocial mold.

Over the years, clang has robbed me of hundreds of nights of refreshing, healing, necessary sleep. Hundreds of my neighbors, who must try to sleep in even closer proximity to clang's metallic clamor, are similarly deprived and damaged. And thousands of other nocturnal innocents are prodded and pushed, against their wills and to their detriment, into bleary-eyed, head-throbbing wakefulness by clang's unruly clan. At a conservative estimate, my own losses by virtue of autointoxication, lack of control, increased irritability, errors at work, decline in spirits, and other well-documented effects of chronic sleep deprivation would have to be multiplied by tens of thousands to approach the scope of clang's wanton destructiveness. Being awakened occasionally in a large city is not unacceptable. But knowing, each time you prepare to go to sleep, that you will probably be awakened unnecessarily because of the indifference or incompetence of others, is punishing. Clang's misdeeds have scarcely been noted, and few are aware of the rising volume of poison steadily seeping into the community bloodstream from this source.

The principal reason clang and his fellows have remained at large so long is that they do their work insidiously. By the time clang's victims have been roused from their slumbers, clang is hunkered down, silently waiting until they have dozed before rising up again. A truck gearing down? Or up? A motorcycle? An ambulance or fire engine? Perhaps a milk delivery. Very few suspect the real culprit. And of the few who know the truth, virtually none has ever accepted clang's rasping challenge head to head, one on one.

When I picked up clang's brazenly thrown down gauntlet, I was characteristically optimistic about the ability of a single, determined, and knowledgeable person to improve the system. I called Con Ed at 212 MU 9-9898 and demanded clang be muzzled. When I persisted, Ed finally dispatched somebody and clang was silenced, not that anybody called back to inform me. When I became aware clang had been subdued, I was elated. As my nervous system gradually became deconditioned to the clang effect, I was able to lengthen my ration of continuous sleep. Before long I could reach daybreak, and even later, without awakening once.

And then it happened! Clang was loose again! I knew it

the moment I was awakened shortly after 3 A.M. Clang, openly defiant, no longer hunkered down. He had gotten me up and was chortling metallically, while my head ached and the stomach acid flowed. I was immediately faced with a Hobson's choice: absorb this latest loss and try to salvage some additional sleep while I still could or become fully aroused, lose another night's sleep, vent my displeasure at Ed, and try to close with clang and silence his taunting forever. The latter action was more my style.

The man who finally answered my call took the information matter-of-factly, a bit too much so for my taste, as I made clear. Why hadn't the original crew silenced clang permanently? They had probably put in a "liner" eliminating the space under clang so clang couldn't be depressed, but sufficient traffic and vibration had displaced the liner enough to give clang some play. I demanded something permanent for clang and was told it would be taken care of, but was given no specifics.

Over approximately the next two years clang more than held his own. I made seven attempts to cage clang; all failed. Each time, over my expressed objections, a liner was the ineffective means Con Ed selected. After a brief tussle, clang shrugged off each inadequate attempt. Clank/ CLANG; clank/CLANG! It was becoming a knell.

In the next encounter, Con Ed delayed more than usual in getting to the job, while I railed and reeled and dosed myself with megavitamins. I kept my own counsel but silently vowed that if Con Ed failed again, I would pry clang out of the ground with my bare hands and bury him at sea one darkling night! I waited for the match between Ed and clang. When it was postponed to the limits of my endurance (megavitamins can only do so much), I began to consult with Ed's handlers. Astonishingly, Ed had taken on a relative of clang, a quiet, well-behaved square cover (clang, of course, is round) that lived fifty yards up the block from clang and had poured "Mac" over the wrong cover. Clang's boisterous chortling continued to echo in my head, but I had vowed to meet clang on the battlefield personally only if Ed finally failed. Ed would be given a last chance.

I arranged to meet with an Ed foreman and let him observe clang making a public nuisance of himself. In my presence, he radioed a steam foreman, who promised to come right over and silence clang forever. I had my doubts but didn't voice them. When nothing had been done three hours later (near midnight) clang was becoming more disorderly, I again demanded action from Ed. Desperate, I was on hand when the steam crew arrived a short time later.

Slavishly repeating their past error, they again attempted to muzzle clang with a liner, despite my demand for a new casting. This time the company, using the same ingenuity and resourcefulness that forced it to eliminate the dividend on its stock a while back, while it was charging the highest rates in the country, installed a liner that was completely useless. Even as the foreman was telling his office the job was satisfactorily completed from a pay telephone a few yards away, clang was chortling his disdain, loudly mocking Ed and me. I pointed this out to the foreman, who ignored me and continued to chat amiably with his office. I couldn't be sure, but I thought I detected a more defiant note from clank.

Beaten and puffy-eyed, but not yet defeated, I returned to my apartment and spoke with the highest ranking employee I could find at that hour, a general foreman. He seemed conscientious and assured me, after I related how inept and deceptive a job had been turned in by his people, that I would get a night's sleep. I, in turn, assured him that if clang were not silenced within an hour, I would check into a hotel—or a hospital—and send the bill to Ed. A few minutes later two barricades and a pair of flashing amber lights were erected about clang and the innocent, square cover that had already been dumped on needlessly. I thought this was a prelude to replacing clang with another casting, which I had insisted on, but I was wrong again.

Fourteen hours into the next afternoon the barricades remained, creating an embarrassing and dishonorable stand-off with clang, and at the price of choking and clotting traffic. I called for help from the day shift. This time clang would be silenced or face a watery grave regardless of what it cost me!

The president of Con Ed was not "in" to my call, which came as no surprise since Jimmy Carter is about the only president I know of who takes calls from the public. And so on down the line deep into the top executive tier, but I would never quit now. High noon or midnight, it was clang or me! Relentless, with the adrenalin in full flow, I was now gaining on clang with every move.

Pressing up, down, and sideways, draining my slender resources heedlessly, I finally succeeded in getting one of my calls returned by a gentleman in charge of the entire metropolitan area, who had been paged in the field. I explained the situation as coherently as I could. I told him there were two problems now: silencing clang—and that could be done only by changing the casting to one that fit— and damages.

He parried the latter by suggesting I write to the house law firm. I explained that as I usually bill about $150 an hour for my time, to compose a careful letter to lawyers seemed a needless, prohibitive expense. He asked whether I wanted him to take the money out of his own pocket. I replied that that would be acceptable if the amount were, but that if he cared to, he could check Ed's records, speak with the people I had (all the incoming calls are recorded), and when he became convinced I had been damaged, make a civilized offer, which I'd accept. He solemnly assured me clang would be silenced shortly and he would call the following day about the offer. He never called back but my escalation of demands put greater pressure on the real problem, as I expected it would.

Within an hour, from my window I saw a crew hard at work on the wrong cover. What did they have against clang's square relative? I joined the crew and told them they were working on the wrong cover. One of the three executives in business suits who were supervising the crew replied.

"You're Mr. Charell," said he, extending his hand. "I'm A— B—."

A short time later the crew had demolished the entire area about clang, the square cover, and another, closer relative of clang on the far corner, which I had pointed out also required attention. This time, three barricades and flashing lights were left standing but the street was eventually smoothed.

The barriers are down now, the flashing amber lights gone. King clang is caged, quiet at last, and apparently subdued, but for how long? How can I ever trust clang's intentions or Ed's competence after all that's gone before? The long struggle has cost me dearly. The residual effects remain all too palpable. I know the result, which looks like victory, is only a temporary standoff. And I know I won't rest easily until clang is melted down and cast into a hundred smaller, more manageable pieces and shipped to Zanzibar or Uch.

12 Positioning

Jerzy Kosinski had a hybrid military uniform made for him that was designed to imply high, nonspecific rank in a nonspecific branch of an unspecified country's military service. When he wore it he was showered with deference, courtesies, and preferences wherever he went. Dick Cavett contrived to meet Jack Paar in an NBC corridor and used a *Time* magazine envelope as a prop to imply he was a *Time* reporter, thereby improving his position with Paar. Young men have been carrying medical bags and stuffing stethoscopes into an outer pocket carelessly for years in an effort to gain access to the hospital rooms of female friends after visiting hours. Applicants for bank loans try to look as prosperous as they can. These and other forms of positioning are intended to confer standing, status, or rank on the positioner. Most of us indulge in one form of it or another on occasion, whether or not we wear uniforms or use props.

Positioning is sometimes done on another's behalf. Attorneys and agents often use this method to secure better terms and conditions for a client or other principal. An advance man smooths the way for the candidate. For generations opera singers have paid claques to applaud wildly and shout approbation. Comedians, booked on important talk shows, are even hiring professional laughers. Staged media events were a commonplace in the late sixties. Executive secretaries sometimes jockey and feint one another into putting the other executive on the telephone first, thereby creating an assumed loss of status for the waiting executive and a corresponding gain for the other.

We are positioned every day in every sensory way. Muzak is said to increase production in certain repetitive factory operations. Appeals to the olfactory sense are being impregnated into print advertising. "Canned" laughter cues us that television comedies are funny. Settings predispose us to act favorably or unfavorably toward others. We assume the person on the throne is royalty and act accordingly. Shipboard acquaintances are accorded special courtesies. Jewels placed on a black velvet background seem more attractive. Poorly dressed professionals tend to lose a measure of standing in our eyes. And panhandlers have begun to take coaching in acting and makeup in order to increase their incomes.

Most of us are willing to play by the rules when we venture forth into social and commercial dealings every day. We lower our voices in funeral parlors and courtrooms and smile for wedding photographers. But when the rules are suddenly changed, we are upset and at a loss. For example, when we enter a crowded bakery we are content to take a ticket numbered in consecutive ascending order, but if, as our number is approached, the salesclerks begin to call the numbers in a random order, we become confused and angry. It is precisely at moments when we are not receiving our due that positioning may be most usefully employed. Although I have always been reluctant to use positioning to give me an *advantage* in an otherwise neutral situation, I have less hesitancy about its use in a situation in which I have been unfairly *dis*advantaged. I find this defensive form of positioning agreeable since I can use it to help restructure an encounter in which I am temporarily one down. I have developed a number of approaches to defensive positioning, which are admittedly rudimentary, even primitive, but they may provide a point of departure, and all have been effective.

I noticed, for example, when I got involved in trying to find remedies for my own justified consumer complaints, that I was sometimes being treated condescendingly. I disliked hearing statements that began with "I'm sorry, but we can't ..." (which usually meant "We choose not to") and ended with "You'll have to ..." followed by some tedious order. In most cases, these orders would have been prohibitively time-consuming to carry out, and I was already at a loss by virtue of some failure of performance on the part of the other side of the transaction. Such comments as "You'll have to bring it in if you expect us to do anything about it and I'm not making any guarantees until we see it," or "You'll have to write us a letter ..." seemed harsh and out of place under those circumstances, particularly as I usually dealt with high-priced shops I considered reliable. It was not the policy of the commercial establishment to treat its customers that way; more often than not it was a particular individual's reaction to hypoglycemia or an unhappy domestic situation, or some other cut or scrape of no direct relevance to the matter at hand. Whatever the source of the difficulty there seemed little point in my taking its brunt.

To imply that it was worth their while to give me their best efforts, and to eliminate as quickly as possible as much of the bad attitude as I could, I often countered firmly and evenly with "I usually bill between $100 and $150 an hour for my time and there is no way I can possibly break even on this transaction." This enhanced my status, since only certain people bill for their time by the hour, and only a few at these rates, and it emphasized my mounting losses in the matter at hand. When I found the other's attitude especially overbearing, I sometimes added "And I know your time is valuable, too," giving the demanding one a better perspective from which to view our interaction. At that point, if I requested a messenger be dispatched to pick up the defective item at once or suggested somebody of higher authority be consulted (naming that person was of help), the matter was usually quickly and satisfactorily concluded, and some warmth was able to waft back into the conversation even as heat was removed.

Sometimes I countered with "You're speaking to a very angry attorney." Few people in the wrong, I discovered, have much desire to converse with irate lawyers at great length, so satisfactory solutions were usually facilitated by that small positioner. Putting a service person on his mettle with "Would it be possible . . . ?" often got a nettlesome matter resolved rather quickly. And appeals to honor ("In all fairness!") were surprisingly effective, even among the less than completely honorable.

A standard opening in a complaint situation was to introduce myself pleasantly and to inquire as to the name of the person with whom I was speaking: "My name is Ralph Charell. May I ask what is your name?" This unthreatening question, asked before any impasse had been reached, was usually answered with a name. If the person at the other end of the line refused to identify himself at that stage, there was little point in continuing the conversation, for by the refusal or evasion I concluded the person was not likely to be responsive and responsible. Playing back their names a couple of times usually had an ameliorating effect. If a satisfactory agreement could not be reached quickly, I would call the person by name and say that if he or she were unwilling or unable to correct the company's error, perhaps I should take the matter up with the store manager, and I would mention the name of that weighty and authoritative— from the point of view of the person with whom I was speaking—person. I would sometimes add that I hadn't wanted to take the time because I usually bill between $100 and $150 an hour for my time, and there was no way I could possibly break even on this unsatisfactory transaction. Primitive? True, but when a reliable company is in the wrong it shouldn't take too much positioning to nudge it into a righteous path.

As it is a statistical fact that impressive stationery is given more weight than less expensive, ordinary letter paper, I used Tiffany & Co.'s ecru with a kid finish and brown stamping to good effect. Occasionally, however, when recalcitrance was encountered, I chose to use a scrap of almost anything at hand, graced it with a practically unintelligible scribble and a few ink blots (rarely seen in this ball point era) so that the missive looked as if it might have been composed by a member of some subhuman species. When personally addressed to an upper-echelon executive, this appeal would typically be passed to an underling with instructions to get such a person off the superordinate's back. The best way, of course, for the high-ranking individual never again to hear from the species member was for the subordinate to satisfy the sloppily drafted but heartfelt request.

Any mention of the word "doctor" in a hospital tends to put the staff at attention. A man I know found himself practically forgotten during his convalescence in a hospital room until he began to call the staff on his floor on the telephone and make requests in the name of Dr. Whatever's office that he be looked in on regularly.

Only a fool or a dedicated masochist would mistreat a sumo wrestler. His prodigious size and strength are evident, and he is accordingly given a wide berth and treated with dignity. We of lesser girth and greater anonymity are rarely attended with smiles and bows; yet are we any less entitled to full measure? Until some universally honored insignia denoting our right to be treated as a fellow human being is struck and pinned on us, the friendly persuasion of defensive positioning, discreetly applied, will continue to provide welcome relief.

13 Parental Guidance

A hundred years ago when our country was growing up commercially, people dealt with one another in a personal, face-to-face way. They went to the general store and the owner waited on them personally and they called one another by name. Later, when the large mail-order companies began to operate, although the transactions weren't done in person they retained elements of this personal nature. Orders placed from mail-order catalogs were often accompanied by long personal letters, and long personal replies were sent with the merchandise. This important quotient of personal relationship in business transactions is only a charming anachronism today.

Business has become bigger, faster, more impersonal. If we buy an ice-cream cone at the corner store, we are probably dealing with a company owned by a giant, computerized conglomerate listed on the New York Stock Exchange. And the people who operate big businesses are employees, not owners. They get paid whether they do a good or a bad job and their salaries are not directly related to sales and profits. The stockholders, who are the real owners, worry about sales and profits but their control of the business is illusory since they rarely vote against management in sufficient numbers to make a difference. Job turnover, competition, transience, mobility, and the remoteness of top management from the actual site of the transaction all add to the process which seals out the personal element from business dealings. And as increasingly complex machines program us to interact with them on their terms, there often isn't even an unresponsive human being on the other side of a business dealing.

The craftsman's pride has been buried in an avalanche of mass-produced goods and the traditional service callings are all but extinct in this country. Who then will listen to us when it is our turn to receive one or another of the twin jokers of "quality control" or "customer service"?

We have seen how to reach and motivate Mr. Big if his subordinates have failed to put right our justified complaint. But what if Mr. Big is indifferent or unreasonable? In one such situation, my wife and daughter bought a piece of furniture and an item included on the signed receipt for that purchase was not shipped with it. After obtaining no satisfaction from anybody else at the store, I reached Mr. Big, a vice president of the company. For reasons I can only assume went far beyond the matter at hand, Mr. Big took a personal interest in frustrating my efforts.

I succeeded by calling the store switchboard and asking whether the store were part of a larger company. It turned out to be owned by a conglomerate listed on the Big Board. As more and more companies are becoming subsidiaries or divisions of larger companies, this approach is increasingly useful. The next call went to the parent company. I asked to speak with the chief corporate counsel and was soon in conversation with a charming and understanding man. I opened by telling him he was speaking with an angry attorney (which tends to put the listener on the defensive). We had been treated outrageously, I explained briefly, and asked what he would do if his wife and daughter had been dealt with as mine had. We were soon chuckling at the behavior of the store vice president, and later that day the attorney arranged for the missing item to be delivered by van, gift-wrapped.

Sometimes the mere mention of the name of the chief executive of the conglomerate is all that is required. But it won't have much effect if you don't get it exactly the way his associates use it. If they call him Harold and you say Harry, forget it.

My wife and I flew down to an offshore island on some business. Our short stay at one of the hotels was like a modern auto-da-fe. Weakened from sleep deprivation caused by the slapping of palm fronds against our terrace railings, commencing a bit after 5 A.M., we were further reduced by missing three consecutive meals through a series of assorted foul-ups. The last meal we missed involved some room-service lobsters (we were conserving energy by lying on our beds), which we were told the chef had agreed to prepare for us, despite the lateness of the hour. We had returned from the hotel dining room of this island paradise after we'd learned that only barbecued food (heavily charcoaled, possibly carcinogenic) was available that night. However, when we called room service we were told it was too late for cooked food. The lobsters arrived at about 11 P.M., uncooked and inedible. Upon inquiry, we were told the chef had decided to retire, after all. Lying on our beds close to exhaustion, we realized we had to check out as soon as we were physically able to do so.

When the palm fronds awakened me early the next morning (by then I had learned to anticipate being awakened and it made the little sleep permitted me uneasy), I tried to get something to eat but had to wait a few hours until the kitchen opened. On checking out, I discovered the hotel had surcharged us 25% on about $200 worth of long distance telephone calls I'd made, adding, without notice, about $50 to the bill for dialing seven telephone numbers. I went to see the hotel manager. When I finished the list of grievances I told the manager I couldn't believe a responsible businessman like Mr. Biggest in the conglomerate chain of command had any idea how this hotel was being run.

No sooner had that sentence been enunciated than the manager asked me to do him a personal favor by permitting him to cancel the entire bill. Within an hour of granting that permission, we were regaining our strength on the terrace of our four-room suite at an ocean club, enjoyably breaking our fast while overlooking some of the bluest water in the western hemisphere.

For those irritating times when our best efforts to redress a justified grievance with a company that is part of a larger company are unavailing, satisfactory and astonishingly swift results are often available at the parent company. Information as to whether there is a parent company and where and whom to call is easily obtainable from a stockbroker, a public or private library, or from the switchboard of the company that refused to cooperate. So, when Mr. Big and Company act like spoiled children, desired results can be produced by providing an opportunity for parental guidance.

14 A Bad Beef

My wife and I visited a resort hotel with two other couples one winter. We'd had an enjoyable stay there some years earlier. Tropical sun was a welcome alternative to ice and freezing rain but the hotel was in something of a decline. Although the rates were higher than ever, many of the gracious touches were missing and the food was no longer excellent.

The grounds were as lovely as we'd remembered and the miles of beautiful beaches hadn't changed. The sky was its wonted bright blue and the sun was undimmed. The ocean was a delight and some of my most relaxing and enjoyable hours were spent snorkling among schools of fish, some of which were startling shades of purple and green and yellow. But the meals suffered from all too obvious cost-cutting. Ordinarily, we might have been able to make other dining arrangements but we were with four other people. Such arrangements would have been unwieldy and we didn't want to upset the others or detract from their enjoyment.

After experiencing, without much comment in deference to our friends, a number of disappointing meals and a Sunday buffet brunch that was a poor shadow of past hospitality, I ordered an end cut of roast prime ribs of beef one evening and was served a cheaper cut, which the captain insisted was prime. I had no wish to disquiet the others at the table by pressing it further, but it rankled. When dinner was over I spoke with the hotel manager, who professed to be unaware of any difference in the quality of the food, which he insisted was the finest money could buy. The alleged roast prime ribs, which I'd had bagged and showed him, were prime, of course, and nothing else. He was unctuous, polite, even courtly, but he was lying and I knew I couldn't let it end there.

It wouldn't be easy to obtain any satisfaction under these circumstances. It was their turf; I wasn't even in my own country. It was their staff, their land, and their food and they seemed to own even the town itself. One of the wealthiest and most powerful family names in the world was associated with the hotel. They had, in short, all of the high ground and I had only the merest handhold. It was a challenge.

The most obvious way to take some of the controls away from somebody who seems to enjoy total control is to enlist outside intervention. But in this case, meat inspectors or the courts, or some other agency of government offered little comfort. Even if I were to receive an immediate, impartial hearing, the hotel could easily stack the deck. And if I proved my case, what then? Our vacation would be a shambles and we would have caused our friends a great deal of distress. And how would this have given us better food?

The other ordinary option of not doing any further business with a particular company that acts unfairly was unavailing here, too, for there were others to consider and we had no wish to upset anybody by leaving. I sought a better result than that, anyway. I began to consider what possible area of the hotel wasn't under the complete control of management. If I could somehow wrest control of some small area it might provide room enough into which to place a lever. In a few moments I had the answer. The old Trojan horse was about to be wheeled out and updated.

I walked to the front desk and requested a safety deposit box. The bag containing the questionable roast beef was torn apart and the contents placed atop the bag inside the box. The safety deposit box had two locks and two keys. The hotel kept one of the keys; I held the other. Our mutual cooperation and presence was the rule in unlocking and locking the box, and I had the privacy of the area during the interval. I called for the deskman and we both solemnly turned our respective keys in their respective locks, placing the roast beef in safekeeping.

Within a short time there was an unmistakably unpleasant air of decay about the front-desk area and I received a call. To the request to empty the box I calmly replied that the box contained valuable evidence that had to remain in safekeeping. This may have puzzled the caller for I soon received a call from the manager. This time it was he who requested a meeting and I was happy to oblige.

The manager asked that I remove whatever was in the

box. He was told the box contained very valuable evidence that could not be disturbed for some time. After further polite conversation which restated his demand and my refusal, he told me that if I didn't remove what I had in the box, the hotel would do so. I pointed out that I had the other key to the box and that if the box were tampered with in my absence, there would be grave legal consequences.

"What do you want?" he finally inquired and I was ready with the answer.

"A roast prime ribs dinner tonight and one for anybody at our table who cares to join me and a couple of bottles of wine, with your compliments."

"And you'll throw out whatever is in the box?"

"Directly after dinner."

Smiling broadly, he stuck out his hand.

That dinner was like old times at the hotel.

15 Wonton Disregard

City life becomes increasingly attenuated and fragile. Herded together physically but otherwise isolated in private membranes of fear and fantasy, megalopolites are at the mercy of others. We are forced to rely for necessities on a grand ballet of teamwork when, in fact, there is no team. There is a growing uneasiness that factions within factions, sacrosanct autonomous pockets demanding much and contributing less and less, will in a crunch deny us the vital linkage for our life supports. Labor unrest, crimes of violence, outages, shortages, and other disruptions, fouled water and air are all too familiar facts of life. And sales of bottled water, firewood, canned goods, and camping equipment are soaring.

These all illustrate the kinds of situations we face each week, in which indifferent individuals who happen to be able to help us simply by doing the uncomplicated jobs for which they were hired, decide, for some reason (or no reason at all) to withhold their goods and services from us despite our need and our ability to pay. Such behavior all too often goes unremarked and unredressed but the resultant frustrations and tensions are left to smolder within. Unexpressed, these feelings are converted into anxiety and act to repress love.

Stunning effects can often be caused by combining two or more separate strategies. Elements of escalation, jeopardy, and surprise, for example, work particularly well in concert, as in the following example. And if the method lacks the soaring majesty of a Gregorian chant, it does provide calm and alkalinity with which to restore the mind's ease and return the stomach's pH to normalcy.

A man came home from the office feeling weak and feverish and, as he put it, "as if someone were exerting thumb pressure on his eyes from the inside." He got undressed and lay down. When the symptoms persisted, he took his temperature. Squinting at the thermometer, he found it to be 102.4.

As time passed he began to get hungry, which he interpreted as a favorable sign. However, as he was a typical young bachelor who rarely ate dinner at home, his cupboard and refrigerator, apart from some coffee and tea, an inch and a half of ketchup and a moldy piece of lemon, were bare. This he interpreted as a bad sign.

At length, from the depths of his tribal memory his feverish mind began to focus on chicken soup as a curative. He wasn't entirely satisfied with the nutritional value of chicken soup, however. Suddenly he had the answer. Wonton soup! Four or five portions of good, health-restoring Wonton soup would tide him over. Although the thumbs were still probing his eyes, he could almost feel himself getting better as he dialed the poshest Chinese restaurant in his neighborhood and, happy coincidence, the only one that delivered.

"Joy Ling," said the voice at the other end of the line.

"I'd like to have some food delivered to my apartment as soon as possible."

"What is the order?"

"Five Wonton soups. Large."

"What else?"

"Nothing."

"Nothing else?"

"No. Just five large Wonton soups. My name is Ross and I'm at 275 North 18th St."

"You are too far away. We don't deliver that far away."

"Well, how far away *do* you deliver?"

"Not past North 17th St."

"But it's only one extra block. Let the delivery person take a cab. I'll pay for it. This is an emergency. I *need* that soup!"

"Too far away. Sorry."

At which point there was a harsh click. The thumbs had become fists and they were no longer simply probing; they were trying to fight their way out. After a while Ross tried again.

"Joy Ling."

"This is Mr. Ross. I was placing an order a few minutes ago and we must have been disconnected."

"You wanted us to deliver some soup?"

"Yes. That's right. Five large Wonton soups. Was I speaking with you?"

"I told you you're too far away. We don't deliver that far."

70

"But it's only one extra block. Let the deliverer take a cab. I'll be happy to pay for it. Both ways."

"You're too far away."

"Look, don't hang up! This is important. I'm sick. I can't go out. I've got an idea. Let's make it worth everybody's time. In addition to the five large Wonton soups I'll have two orders of Chow Ming Young. How can I go wrong with your good beef? Right?"

"You're too far away. We don't deliver past North 17th St."

"Let me talk to the manager."

"I am the manager."

Again there was a click as the conversation was terminated.

That night Ross had some tea and lemon and his condition worsened. While he was recovering his health he would occasionally hear strange clicks, and he found himself drifting out of conversations to brood about Joy Ling's delivery zone. Why did people treat others like that? When would they ever learn to live in harmony with one another? How to even the score? By the time he was well again the method had taken shape in his mind.

"Joy Ling."

"This is Mr. Fleming," said Ross smoothly. "I'd like to have some food delivered."

"What is the order?"

"Well, my wife is having her bridge club over this evening and she's asked me to get plenty of food for 12 people. Maybe you can suggest some house specialties."

"They like lobster?"

"I'm sure some of them do."

"Get two Lobster Soong."

"Fine. Also, 12 Wonton and Egg Drop soups combined. Mix them together, right?"

"You want 12 Wonton and Egg Drop soups mixed together."

"Right. Then six large orders of Spare Ribs and about four orders of Mixed Appetizers. And I'm sure we'll need some beef dishes. Let's see . . . one Beef with Oyster Sauce, one Beef with Chinese Vegetables, one Beef with Snow Peas and one Steak Kew. Then a Wor Shu Duck, one Moo Goo Gai Pan, two Shrimp Lo Mein and two Sweet and Pungent Pork. Also, some rice all around, pineapple for about eight, and Fortune Cookies for everybody. Would you mind repeating the order? . . . Good. My address is 185 North 16th St. About how soon may we expect the order?"

"Well, Mr. Fleming," replied the manager shamelessly, "your wife always has the boy take a cab."

Ross noted the ad-libbed untruth without missing a tempo.

"If my wife always does so, by all means have the boy take a cab."

While the restaurant was allowed sufficient time to make the delivery, Ross heated a can of frozen Wonton soup. Why weren't people more considerate of one another, he wondered. They even seemed to be deliberately colliding with one another on the sidewalk. The time passed quickly and he was soon ready to make his point.

"Joy Ling."

"Let me speak with the manager."

"I am the manager."

"This is Mr. Fleming. What happened to the order?"

"Mr. Fleming, the boy just came back. Nobody knows you at 185 North 16th St."

"That's not surprising because I don't live there and my name isn't Fleming. I called you a few days ago and begged you to send me some soup because I was too sick to come and get it but I was one block too far away. Remember that?"

"Oh yes. North 18th St."

"Two can play the same game, you know. I can do this again, although I don't intend to if you'd be willing to extend your delivery zone one block."

"We could do that."

"Good," said Ross, terminating the conversation with a harsh click in the manager's ear.

"If I ever want their food," mused Ross aloud, "I'll eat it there and pay cash. No point in identifying myself for them. Who knows what they might put in the food."

That night for the first time in weeks, Ross slumbered deeply and without interruption. No more grinding of teeth and rapid eye movements to betray his troubled dreams. In the morning he felt refreshed and well rested and, for the moment, he was at peace with the world.

16 Doors

Mike Malley, a Chicago letter carrier, had been out of phase with doors all day. He'd gone to the corner luncheonette to get the morning paper and some breakfast but found the door locked. Peering through the plate glass, he could see Wilner, a gaunt, serious man, beginning to get the place set up for the day. All of Mike's remonstrating was to no avail. The man refused to admit his hungry customer and, toward the end of the exchange, he'd raised his voice to Mike.

On his way to work, the bus driver, adept from years of practice, closed the door the instant before Mike planned to scramble aboard. As the bus started from the curb, slowly,

Mike, thwarted, danced along outside, gently tapping his fare against the door in a vain effort to play on the better nature of the driver. The latter pretended to be occupied with traffic patterns as he increased his speed deliberately. If Mike hadn't given up after a block and a half, the driver might have been forced to run a red light or skip a stop to elude him.

Later that morning Mike entered a revolving door that was stuck. While he was struggling with it, a porter with a rag ran toward him. The porter, a man of few words, pointed to a side door as he began to polish the hardware on the revolving door he'd jammed. On his way out to lunch, which was actually Mike's first meal of the day, he entered an empty elevator. As he kept pressing the "close" button, other passengers rushed in, one by one, tripping the electric eye and reopening the closing door each time the elevator was at last ready to descend.

That afternoon Mike raced to reach his bank before it closed. Mr. Granek, the kindly bank guard, was locking the door as Mike dashed up.

"Sorry," said Mr. Granek. "You're too late."

"But it's only 2:57," Mike protested, looking at his watch. "Even your own clock doesn't show 3:00 yet. I only want to deposit my paycheck." Mike held up the check almost pleadingly.

"I'm sorry," said Mr. Granek, and he really seemed to be. He was always so good-natured. "Have a nice week-end." Mike walked away, too winded and spent from sprinting to argue further.

On his way home from the post office, Mike stopped off at a boutique to pick up the birthday gift he'd bought for his daughter. He hadn't seen much of her in the two years he and his wife had been separated. Mike had picked out an expensive ski sweater and paid for it. He'd asked the woman to gift wrap it and told her he'd pick it up before the store closed. He'd hurriedly changed into an old pair of pants and a shirt in the post office locker room but now, as he approached the store, he could relax; it was still a few minutes before closing time.

However, when he tried the door it was locked. He rapped on the thick glass door but the woman inside did not respond. As he was pounding on the door, the shop owner (who'd originally sold him the gift) drew up in her car. She'd left to pick up her car and had instructed the clerk not to admit anybody she didn't know.

Once inside his apartment, Mike put the gift on a table and collapsed into a chair. It had been another joyless day. Why was there no feeling of community in the community? Gradually he pulled himself together, heated a TV dinner and ate it watching the seven o'clock news on television. Before long the eleven o'clock news was drawing banteringly to a close. Mike decided to treat himself to some ice cream and there was just enough time to get it before Johnny Carson's monologue.

He threw on some old clothes and headed for the corner luncheonette. Wilner, the owner, had been needlessly uncooperative that morning. Mike hadn't quite gotten over that but he swallowed his pride because Wilner's was the only store in the neighborhood which sold the Louis Sherry ice cream he loved. He always ordered half chocolate, half coffee, packed to order while he waited.

As Mike approached the store, he could see that one of the lights was out but fortunately Wilner was still there. When he arrived, however, the door was locked! And Wilner was sitting in a booth facing the door, counting the day's receipts.

At first Mike hesitated. He didn't want to face the

possibility of being deliberately shut out twice. But the thought of Louis Sherry's chocolate and coffee got the better of him. And besides, there was no time for delay if he didn't want to miss Carson's monologue. Wilner finally finished counting and approached the door.

"Sorry, Mike, we're closed. It's been a long day." He pulled down the long door shade between himself and Mike.

Mike trudged off in his slippers. At an all-night superette, he bought a carton of chocolate and a carton of coffee ice cream. Packaged ice cream was never the same and of course they didn't have Louis Sherry's but he would make do. On the way toward the checkout counter, Mike suddenly brightened. There, not four feet from his hands, was a rack of combination locks. Mike reached for a sturdy one. He had come to that point of circuit overload at which he no longer had any desire whatever for what a moment ago he thought he had to have. Now, the only way to deal with Wilner would be in kind.

Mike quickly padded back to Wilner's and sidled up to the door. Through a small piece of glass left uncovered by the shade, he could see Wilner putting on his jacket preparatory to departing for the night. Mike silently placed the metal hasp over the eye and gently padlocked the door.

Mike put the ice cream out to thaw and turned on the set. He'd missed the monologue but it couldn't be helped. He turned the sound off on a commercial and reached for the telephone.

"Hello," said Wilner. "Who is this?"

"Oh, hello, Mr. Wilner. I'm glad it's you. This is Sgt. Doniger of the 16th precinct," said Mike. "One of our patrol cars reported that your door was locked but somebody was inside."

"I'm glad you called, sergeant. I was just about to call

the precinct. Some lunatic locked me in the store."

"Just sit tight, Mr. Wilner. We've got a couple of patrol cars on the way over right now."

"For God's sake, tell them not to shoot!"

"Don't worry, sir. We'll have you out in no time. But maybe you'd better stay out of sight."

Mike got back to his program. Packaged ice cream wasn't too bad after all.

17   The Big Picture

A maxim that has been given much circulation over the years advises us to "Take care of the little things and the big things will take care of themselves." I recommend the opposite approach. A surprisingly small number of key elements (big things), perhaps three or four, are of controlling importance in almost any situation. These three or four major chunks comprise what I call the big picture, and they should be the focus of our attention. If I am satisfied with the big picture, the rest is of little concern. That is to say, once we've taken care of the big things, the little things will take care of themselves or they won't, but it shouldn't make a great deal of difference.

In the family budget, for example, the big spending chunks involve food, clothing, shelter, and entertainment for most people. If meaningful savings are to be made, they will come from these items. If not, the solution probably lies not in reduced spending but in increased income.

In food packaging, the label is required to indicate the contents in the order of importance by weight. The first three or four ingredients listed usually comprise substantially all of the net weight of the package. If these ingredients are not to our liking there would be no point in buying the package, regardless of how much the other ingredients may be liked or desired.

The most important three or four items in practically any situation we may face will constitute the lion's share. Even the most complicated contracts that may have taken teams of professionals months to negotiate contain only a few crucial elements. In employment contracts, for example, the big chunks for the employee might be how much, how long, to do what, and under what conditions. In a lease, the big picture for the lessee would be which space, how long, how much, for what purpose.

I have sometimes reduced a complex situation to a single question: does this person, this contract, this job make me feel good about myself? This is the big picture for me. If the answer is in the affirmative, I will go to almost any length and make almost any sacrifice to try to get it to fly. But if the answer comes up tails, it has a chilling effect. I have walked away from a couple of careers, a business, and dealings of many descriptions on these bleak occasions, any one of which might have been attractive under more favorable circumstances.

There is greater latitude for negotiating in most situations than is generally recognized. If the big picture is different for the parties on opposite sides of the table, the negotiating process can be simplified. Each will concede what is less important to receive what is more important and both may emerge with the elements they prize most. It is therefore useful to discover what the other party values most in these situations so that the key elements may be traded off. It's a mistake to assume we know this answer. We should probe for it, and, if necessary, ask. And we should always listen carefully for clues as to where the other party's major interests lie. In many situations, even if the parties want the same things, they may have slightly different orders of preference that will facilitate the negotiating, or the elements may be alternated or separated in acceptable ways.

Many employees fail to capitalize on the opportunities inherent in their jobs by not fully understanding what is the big picture of the job they are expected to perform. They may think they understand the nature of the job but they may not appreciate how the person to whom they report views their job. Generally, we should look for the major productive or profitable functions of the job and be alert to how these can be increased or improved and to what other productive and profitable opportunities we can add to the job and the company. The big picture (the key elements) probably bulks about 90% of the entire job picture. This is where the effort should be concentrated. Everything else is of secondary importance and, if possible, may be delegated; otherwise, these secondary items may be bunched or bundled and disposed of in down time.

In personal relationships, the minor irritations are not parts of the big picture. It still surprises me to see people who have been close friends for years suddenly cut each other off over something trivial; or see married couples who separate and divorce over arguments about nonessentials. Presumably, there is much beneath the surface that is unsatisfactory. But if the focus had been on the key elements from the outset, the little things would have been kept small.

If the big picture is a desirable one, insignificant elements should never be permitted to threaten it. For example, if we bicker with our spouses or mates about insignificant matters, perhaps it is time to concentrate on solutions instead of problems. If one spouse is a bad cook, for example, there are many constructive approaches to be considered calmly. The other might try cooking an occasional meal or participating in preparing some of the meals. That individual might volunteer to do some other household chores in order to provide more time for the "bad" cook to do the cooking. You both might consider hiring outside help to do some of the cooking or housekeeping. You might eat more meals in restaurants or exchange dinner party invitations with friends. Either or both of you might want to improve your cooking skills by taking a class. Both of you might want to simplify the meals you eat at home. There are dozens of ways of approaching the problem once you both agree on its relative unimportance compared with the desirable big picture.

The big picture is a reliable guide that leads to enthusiasm and wholeheartedness. By taking care of the big things, we improve our chances for providing an environment in which we may grow and develop. At the same time, we keep the little things from becoming magnified out of proportion.

18　Getting it for Less

Some people know how to get almost everything they buy for practically nothing. Even wholesale isn't good enough; they want it at less than cost. And then they're not always happy. They'd prefer to take an item they're about to throw out and trade it for a flatcar of silk purses. I know somebody like that who traded an old undistinguished camera into a luxury motorboat in about two years.

These people may be observed rummaging through warehouses of distressed goods, casually picking up heirlooms for a few cents a pound. They break bread and exchange anecdotes with captains of tramp steamers bound for exotic destinations on the other side of the globe. Total out of pocket: something like a few bars of "Melancholy Baby." Occasionally, they come into truckloads of priceless treasures for the mere cost of hauling them away. Or they may stumble onto native handcrafts wrought of ivory and gold, a boatload of which they trade for a few hand mirrors and some cigarette lighters.

They travel from one bargain basement and discount store to another, buying out of season merchandise in clearance sales. Or they make the rounds of discount stores, thrift shops, Salvation Army stores, and charity bazaars, furnishing their apartments for less than the cost of an ordinary meal. They regularly cast a wary eye on closeout opportunities, liquidation sales, and "cents-off" coupons. They devote much time to this occupation, for buying at retail is taboo, and they even know how and where to buy postage stamps at a discount from collectors whose anticipated profits on hundreds of sheets of stamps failed to materialize. They are also irresistibly attracted to the word "free" and are continually requesting free samples, entering contests, and filling out and sending off coupons to Battle Creek and Minneapolis by the bushel. And, like central bankers, they keep shifting their funds, claiming a variety of gifts from a long list of savings banks in the process.

I've seen buyers and sellers haggle and bargain with the zest and precision of violin virtuosi, enjoying it as much as a set of tennis, even if no sale results. Scarcely more verbose than mime players, they are able to communicate subtle thoughts and emotions through gesture, facial expression, and breathing. And I am aware that this activity is commonplace, not only at stalls of Arabian bazaars.

But I have no skill at all in getting things at the right price. I manage to pay top dollar, sometimes timing my purchase a couple of days before an item goes on sale at a 30-percent discount. Nor have I the companion skill of hiring a band of needy cooks and chauffeurs and butlers and cleaning people and nannies, and other servants, foreign and domestic, for some ridiculous wage, irregularly paid. I may be difficult to please and sensitive to poor work and bad grace but I never try to adjust the price unless the other side first fails to keep its part of the bargain. I also overtip, excessively handing out currency to an extremely wide variety of service people.

I've wondered why I continually pay service and tradespeople and merchants more than I need to when I am a tough, even difficult, negotiator when the other side is a public utility or a large corporation. I think the answer lies in an incident in my childhood. At the height of the Great Depression our family took a vacation with another family. The day we returned home my father and the waiter who had served us during our stay got into a loud argument over a tip. I was only about three or four years old but I remember the scene. Maybe I've been trying to repay that waiter for my father all these years. At any rate, a few words are in order about the time-honored practice of trying to get it for less, which has balanced buyers and sellers in a delicate equation for centuries. Although I have a strong preference for approaching reality from the bedrock of my own concrete experience, in this instance I speak only from firsthand personal observation.

Almost all businesses charge a range of prices for the same goods and services. One price distinction we are all familiar with is that between wholesale and retail, for example. Sometimes this price differential is based on the seller's first impression and this can be influenced in ways that may encourage preferential treatment.

If you enter an electrical supply store and ask for some advice as to what kind of wire you'd need to hook up an appliance in your basement, you will pay the top price and probably be kept waiting. Go into the same store and confidently order "25 feet of 12-2 BX cable" and the bill will be reduced by about 15 percent. Roll up in a panel truck, double-park it outside the store and enter, wearing a shirt with a name embroidered over the pocket, and you save an additional 10 percent. And if you wish to imply you might need a regular supply of large quantities of named staples, mentioning offhandedly your reluctance to bother the store and yourself on an order this small—your regular supplier has let you down—then shamelessly and unblinkingly asking for their card so your purchasing agent may call, the price declines again.

In a camera store, the gambit might go along these lines: You walk in carrying an expensive camera, say a Nikon or Leica, which marks you as serious, particularly if the camera is not in its case. Once you have the attention of the owner or a salesperson who seems to have the authority to make a deal, you find a subtle flaw in a camera you're inspecting, to establish your familiarity with the merchandise: "There's a scratch on the pressure plate and a rattle in the range finder."

This should not be said loudly or in a manner which indicates you are rejecting the camera or questioning the reliability of the store. You don't want the salesperson to react defensively by becoming short with you. You are still interested in buying this camera and are only questioning its price. And you know there's *always* one scratch and one rattle, both insignificant.

If you should then drop the name of a service company used by the local professionals ("I'll have to get BeeZee Service to check this out on the bench") you have placed yourself in a position to be charged the normal professional discount. But you can still prove yourself a tough customer by giving the matter a little extra thought and simply asking "Is that your best price?" Chances are the price will be reduced a last 5 percent, to the lowest the store offers.

Quality, of course, is another matter, and here I must confess, I am very much a player. I'd like to get the best quality I can at a given price. Interestingly, American business has not yet standardized everything, so we can often buy products which vary in quality but not in price. Unhappily, however, although we want the best, we cannot always identify it and are therefore one down against the seller. The solution may not be too difficult.

There is a food store on New York's upper West Side that offers a wide variety of high-quality smoked fish, meats, cheeses, produce, cakes, coffees, teas, and other specialty items. There is only one price for any given item but, as with most food, the quality may vary considerably. As a nonexpert buyer, I was taking home the least choice parts of the various fish and meats offered until I noticed an obviously knowledgeable old woman step up to the counter. She didn't simply order a piece of whitefish; she asked for "A *nice* piece of whitefish; know what I mean, Sam?" And she didn't simply get whatever was on top of the heap, as I had. Sam spent a couple of minutes trying to locate the best piece of fish they had. When he didn't come up with something acceptable right away, the woman prompted him: "A nice middle piece; right, Sam?"

Well, with coaching like that, I've been happy to follow the example of that old pro for years and instead of taking home the tail, as I used to, I've been enjoying a nice middle. And if Sam is good enough for that knowledgeable old woman, he's good enough for me, too.

19 Mind English

"Body English" is defined by the Unabridged Edition of The Random House Dictionary as "Sports, a twisting of the body by a player as if to help a ball already hit, rolled or kicked to travel in the desired direction."

This concept is familiar. We have seen bowlers strain to influence the path of a bowling ball as it approaches the pins. And we have watched batters try to direct the flight of a batted ball that appeared to be curving into the stands foul. Perhaps we can extend this concept of body English to "mind English," which might be defined as "a twisting of the mind of another in the desired direction by a player as if to help a situation apparently booted, missed, or lost."

Individuals react to defeat in many different ways. There are good and bad losers; people who seek out losses compulsively, and others who make futile attempts to avoid losses in ways designed to assure their own defeats. For those who wish another chance when loss or failure looms, one more swing at the ball after they've struck out, I suggest consideration of a new approach, mind English.

Let's say, for example, you've driven into town to keep an important business appointment. You arrive a few minutes early, allowing time to park your car. However, all of the parking lots and garages are full and there is not a single parking space on nearby streets. It has taken you several minutes to develop this unfavorable information and you are now slightly late. You must make a decision at once and your choices are limited.

You have no time to drive to the edge of town and park and hope to find a taxi to take you to your destination; there are no parking spaces available, and you are late. What's your move? People faced with this factual situation ordinarily try to park illegally, risking an immediate towaway in some cities. (In New York this involves a $65 towing charge and a $25 illegal-parking ticket, plus the inconvenience and expense of retrieving the car from its place of impoundment.) I've seen some people jockey their cars into spaces next to fire hydrants and bus stops. Others try to push cars legally parked at corners so that their own vehicle overhangs the building line by only two-thirds of a car length. These obviously vain attempts almost invariably attract parking tickets.

Mind English offers a different card to be played in such situations. Instead of trying to come as close as possible but obviously failing, mind English players would miss the target by a such a wide margin it would change the quality of the act in the mind of the beholder from illegal parking to something else. At best, it would also create the desire to be of help instead of the need to punish. For example, the car might be left in the middle of the street with the hood up and a note on the windshield. The natural assumption would be the car had been overtaken by mechanical failure and broken down, and the driver had gone to call for help. The busier the street and the nearer the middle the car is abandoned, the more believable the ploy.

In an hour, when your meeting is over, you simply waltz over to the car, close the hood, start it up, and drive away. Even if observed leaving, you will probably get the benefit of the doubt, since flooding was always a possibility. A crude example, perhaps, but the Wright brothers were only able to fly a few feet that first day at Kitty Hawk.

Here's another situation. Say you've agreed (against your better judgment) to meet at your office or at luncheon next Wednesday with somebody you've been ducking for a while, but to whom you've now succumbed as an unavoidable courtesy. However, next Monday an engagement for the same time presents itself. You much prefer to take this meeting but it's not good form to simply cancel the earlier appointment in favor of the later opportunity. If you keep the original appointment, you forfeit one much more important to you. If you cancel, you're committing a breach of business etiquette. How do you handle it?

Schedule the meeting you prefer to take at once when it presents itself on Monday. On that same day, you, or better your secretary, calls the other person's secretary and confirms the appointment for *Tuesday*. This may create some consternation as the appointment was set for Wednesday. However, the other party may be happy to accommodate the Tuesday appointment. If he's not, you will have an opportunity to reschedule without seeming to be deliberately canceling the original appointment and brutally trampling his ego. You have given him an opportunity to accept the Tuesday meeting time or to reschedule without losing face and, of course, you are free to keep the Wednesday meeting of greater importance.

Mind English can also be helpful in a number of other typical situations. You're on a tight schedule and have only a few minutes to get from your office to another meeting shortly after five on a Friday afternoon. It's the height of rush hour traffic and taxis are in great demand and short supply. Instead of darting in and out of traffic trying in vain to beat all comers to the occasional empty cab that approaches, you might try to attract the taxi to you by carrying one or two empty pieces of luggage. Alert cab drivers will assume you are bound for the airport and skid to a screeching halt beside you. When you are comfortably seated, simply give the driver your destination and, as the signs say, "sit back and relax."

What would you do if you suddenly remembered a meeting you were supposed to attend two hours ago? There is no way you could suddenly appear, even if the meeting were still in progress. You would be considered boorish and arrogant and your effectiveness at the meeting would be destroyed. But what if you were to show up at the appointed time a day or a week late? ... And the same approach might be used with forgotten birthdays and weddings.

More subtle and refined variations of mind English await the analyses of future pioneers. It is sufficiently rewarding for us to validate the theory and its primary applications and move on to chart other trails in the wilderness.

20 Reading the Fine Print

Telephone company operators were once polite and eager to be of help, the service was good, and the bills were small. Not any more. Despite much self-serving advertising and publicity, ordered by the company (and paid for by us), to the effect that it costs less to make certain calls than it used to, our bills and the company's profits and dividends keep mounting. And while we're paying more money, we seem to be receiving more hostility, discourtesy, uncorrected failures of performance, and less candor.

Getting credits for various improper automatic charges, for example, is a good deal less than automatic, I've discovered. If I experience difficulty on a call and I report it for credit by dialing 211, I will be told: "Credit has been given." In fact, "Credit has been given" actually turns out to mean credit has *not* been given but that credit has merely been applied for. Only if "certain minimum criteria are met" (nobody has yet explained to me what these criteria are), credit *may* be given at a later time. Therefore, to routinely tell a customer that credit has been given when it has not and may or may not be given in the future is deceptive.

Meeting these "minimum criteria" (which the company has presumably set forth somewhere) is only the first hurdle. The company personnel involved must also show sufficient competence to actually give the credit due, which is by no means assured. Any slippage, any error, and the customer is the loser. And if the credit we were led to believe "has been given" is not subsequently given, we are never informed, nor are we told the reason for this denial or given any opportunity to rebut it. And there is no separate line on our bill to indicate any credits given (or denied). In the case of local message-unit calls it is virtually impossible to tell whether we were actually credited, as the telephone company had informed us we would be. In the case of long-distance calls, unless we do continual bookkeeping (which we have no way of knowing will be necessary), we won't know which credits for company failure we have been denied.

Another little known fact about the credits given is this: "In cases where a customer claims that there was poor transmission during a call, a standard one-minute adjustment is made unless the customer indicates the call was longer in duration." It is doubtful one telephone user in a thousand is aware of this arbitrary limitation and surely the company knows the precise length of long-distance calls. Why is it necessary for the customer to "specifically indicate that the call was longer in duration" than a minute? And if it is necessary, why doesn't anybody ask us instead of automatically limiting the credit to one minute's worth of the call?

Say, for example, we're on a business call, the formalities are all out of the way and we're getting to the nub of the deal, when we're disconnected by some mechanical failure of the telephone company. By the time we call back our party is on another call. We then have to leave for a meeting. We will never regain the timing on this deal and it may actually cost us thousands of dollars. If we apply for credit, we may get back 35¢ of a $6 charge for the call but we're in no mood to ask for the credit even if we think of it later. The net result is that if we ask for credit, we may get nothing or a few pennies; if we don't ask, we get nothing. Either way we lose. No wonder the dividend keeps going up! Who's protecting the public?

A few subscribers, of course, do get excellent service. When I was employed by one of the television networks, the building continually swarmed with telephone company installers and repair people. When a problem arose, a secretary would make an interoffice call. Before long, the familiar face of a repairer would appear at the door, tool kit in hand, instruments dangling from a belt. Service was quickly restored and the repairer would be off to the jungle of wires behind panels on another floor. Telephone company personnel were on the premises daily to maintain the company's lines of communication. Of course, the network's total telephone company charges were probably up around eight figures annually.

When I left the network I set up a little company of my

own. While my annual telephone bills are only four figures, my telephone service is as important as it was. Perhaps more so, for I used to have access to other lines if mine failed. In addition, I wasn't the principal source of all the network's revenues. If my lines weren't working, the rest of the company could continue to do business. But in my own company, if my lines didn't function I would soon be out of business. Nevertheless, although I didn't expect to receive such extraordinary service for my own small company, I did expect relief from malfunctions and, of course, candor. I didn't get either.

The chronic difficulties on my telephone included all of the following problems, and often two or three of them at once: mechanical failures that prevented me from making calls; other failures that made it impossible to receive calls; failures to credit my account properly; crackling on the line; crossed lines; the elimination of alternate syllables of a conversation so that all attempts to communicate were frustrated; disconnection of conversations; faulty relays; wrong numbers reached although correctly dialed; howling noises; echoes; whistling noises; and various other failures. When I periodically asked the company to remedy the various problems, the typical response was a claimed inability to find the cause.

After wearying months of unresolved difficulties, I asked for a hearing before the New York State Public Service Commission (PSC). I set forth the list of problems, the company responded, and a PSC man was sent to investigate my lines in the presence of a telephone company employee. The fact that many of the problems I had alleged had actually been heard by named telephone company personnel on my lines was not enough. The PSC insisted on conducting its own check of my lines. What, I asked, if no problems were encountered on a few calls made during part of a single day? The answer from the PSC was vague, but ominous.

On September 15, 1976 the PSC investigator and the telephone company representative arrived. Eight test calls were made to three people in Los Angeles, San Francisco, and Las Vegas. Two calls came in from Chicago and Los Angeles, which I turned over to the PSC man without comment to the callers, asking the man to inquire as to whether the callers had experienced difficulties in speaking with me on my telephones.

All five of these people told the PSC man they had encountered a multiplicity of problems over a long period of time in trying to speak with me on my lines. And of the eight calls made by the PSC man, two were faulty. One call exhibited "clipping," the elimination of intermittent syllables of the conversation. After being dialed, the other call took more than three minutes—timed by the PSC investigator—to go through. I thought the next step would be for the company to refund some of the money I had been overcharged for the years of inadequate telephone service for which I had been paying the full price.

The PSC hearing officer informed me in a letter that further tests of my lines were made from a point outside our premises:

> Staff subsequently placed a number of test calls to western coast states in order to test for clipping or voice suppression. It was confirmed that in calls to certain western states the conversation of distant parties could in effect be "shouted down" by the calling party on the East Coast. Staff has subsequently determined that this voice suppression is due to the use of echo suppressors in the network. An echo suppressor is basically a pair of voice-operated switchers which,

while one subscriber is talking, insert a loss of 35 db. or more in the echo return path. In case both parties talk simultaneously, the talker whose signal is stronger at the echo suppressor will control the switch and he will be heard. Although they effectively suppress echoes, echo suppressors can introduce transmission impairments by sometimes clipping the beginning of words. The "clipping" reported by Mr. Charell is thus a characteristic of the trunking network resulting from the use of echo suppression, and is not a service impairment related to his service. Therefore, no credit can be recommended for this condition.

Nice bit of reasoning there by the PSC hearing officer— even better, in fact, than the explanation the telephone company's legal department had given. The PSC had impartially determined that I was able to hear only intermittent parts of conversations on a fair percentage of long distance calls, as I had alleged. However, the hearing officer determined no credit for this condition (which had cost me lots of money and nerve endings) could be recommended because he defined it as "not a service impairment." It's a service *enhancement*, I suppose. Significantly, the New York State Public Service Commission has no jurisdiction over long lines. And, as I'd stated, entire conversations, not just the beginnings of words, were clipped and nobody was "shouted down"; the clipping occurred without any response at all from me. Nobody explained why this condition occurred only "sometimes." Nor did anybody tell me that after trying in vain to understand somebody whose conversation was clipped, if I asked for credit for the call, which was only occasionally, I would be getting credit for one minute, if that. And why was the New York State PSC hearing officer deciding a matter that lay outside his jurisdiction?

At the hearing I'd said that my payments to the telephone company totalled several thousand dollars per year. Not only was I being damaged in my business by chronic poor service but I was clearly paying for good service and getting poor service. Forgetting the damages, wasn't I entitled to a rebate of some of the money I'd spent? Sounded reasonable, even generous, to me. Bottom-line recommendation from the PSC: zero.

The Federal Communications Commission, on my application, asked the telephone company to respond to my allegations, which it did. "In cases where a customer claims that there was poor transmission during a call, a standard one-minute adjustment is made unless the customer specifically indicates that the call was longer in duration." The answer alleged that additional test calls were made by the company from three central offices (not from my premises, not using my equipment, not with the PSC or myself present). "No difficulties were experienced or troubles found on any of these calls." Were you surprised?

I had repeatedly asked to have my telephone sets exchanged for other equipment, which would have been extremely easy to accomplish, as all of our telephones are on plugs which fit into jacks. The company replaced one of my wife's private telephones but repeatedly refused to exchange any of the business telephones, the lines that produced most of the troubles and account for the bulk of the charges and most of the damages.

It was certainly not unlikely many of the problems stemmed from our equipment and the best way to eliminate this as a possible cause was to replace the telephones. After all, when our lines had been tested outside our premises by the company, they reported no problems, whereas when my equipment had been tested by the PSC, two of eight calls were faulty.

The company also steadfastly refused to rewire our jacks. I learned that the wiring in jacks may include an upper pair, a lower pair, or both pairs of wires. If only one pair of wires is connected to a jack, only some plugs will enable a subscriber to place outside calls; if the wrong plug is used, the line will fail to produce a dial tone. However, if both pairs of wires are connected, any plug will work and the telephones may be interchanged at will. As I'd originally requested this capacity to interchange telephones at will and the company had wired my various lines with only one pair of wires, I asked they be rewired.

With much persistence, and at about the speed of orthodontia, we were able to prevail on the company to replace our telephones and to rewire the jacks. By a happy "coincidence," from the day our telephones were replaced there has been no more "clipping." The only remaining problem is that the company has yet to reimburse us for our overpayments during the period of the extremely poor service. We will request a hearing from the Federal Communications Commission and if this is unavailing, we will, with great reluctance, proceed in the courts.

I believe this company is losing the confidence and good will of large segments of the public. One index of antipathy is the striking statistic that shortly before mail was no longer delivered postage due, as many as thirty percent of telephone bills on the Pacific Coast were being sent in without postage.

There are several reasons for this residue of bad will. The "message unit" has been introduced, which allow the company to divide a local call into several parts and charge for every part instead of a single charge for a single local call. And the basic bill includes only fifty of these greatly devalued "units" instead of seventy or more calls, as in the past. We get less; we pay more and more. The nickel call is twenty cents in North Carolina. In Southern California, a call for directory assistance gets an annoying little lecture before the information is given.

The company has also been permitted to introduce an extra charge for directory assistance. The white pages of telephone directories used to be printed four columns to the page; now there are five columns on a page and the type is correspondingly smaller. No, we're not all suddenly losing our sight; the type is much smaller. This means that while the company is saving on printing and distribution costs, we're all being charged millions of dollars because we're simply unable to read the new small type comfortably. And if a single digit is misread, we will reach a wrong number.

When I raised this point with the New York State PSC, I was told this "has been reviewed by the Commission in the formal case on directory assistance." Maybe it's time for another review. I was also told this extra charge was an advantage for lots of people because if they didn't use directory assistance they received a small credit. My reply was that if the company were not benefiting itself at the public's expense, they would not have introduced the charge or would soon petition for its abolition, which they haven't yet done.

While I wait for the microfiche edition of the telephone directory and the reimbursement of some of the money I overpaid, whenever the spirit moves me I write my check to the company in handwriting the same size as the type in their five-columns-to-the-page directory, to show I haven't lost my sense of humor. And if they or my bank can't read it, I cheerfully refer them to directory assistance.

21   Sign Language

Sometimes words alone, whether spoken or written, may be insufficient to cause the desired effect. But when coupled with a bit of direct action, words may turn a sluggish tide into grand rapids.

A man in New York received a defective item from a furniture company. All of his telephoned and written attempts to resolve the matter with the store brought him only frustration. Nothing, not even a credit or an exchange (the lowest forms of relief) was offered. Store personnel were still being vague and unresponsive months later.

While it may not be the policy of a company to cheat its

customers, the company knows that if ten justified complaints are ignored long enough, or allowed to languish in various culs-de-sac, eventually virtually every one of them will cease to be pressed. In these mercantile matters, justice sufficiently delayed is almost certainly justice denied. And the obstacle course the buyer must run is controlled by the seller. It may be made so difficult that few, if any, last its rigors.

Our man, however, was of a hardy breed. After several months without tangible result, he decided to confront the store *mano a mano*. He lettered a placard with a brief factual message to the effect that the store had "stuck" him with the item specified and he picketed the store. He soon began to draw a crowd. Passersby stopped to chat with him, to encourage him, and to exchange their own tales of bad goods and unhappy endings.

After a while a store employee requested he come inside to discuss the matter. He refused. A few minutes later a store executive invited him inside. The man replied that he'd give the store an opportunity to resolve their differences, but not before he picketed for at least an hour. When the hour elapsed the man entered the store and was taken to see one of the company vice presidents. The latter was polite and extremely apologetic for the way our man had been treated. They both agreed the matter had been very poorly handled and that good help was becoming scarcer. The matter was quickly resolved to the satisfaction of the customer.

In this case, picketing was an effective last resort. However, in some states picketers can be sued for damages. So before going public with a justified complaint, it's important to find out whether it's cricket to picket where you live. If you decide to picket, don't exaggerate or overstate your case; don't disparage the store, only the particular item you bought; don't threaten or be coercive; and don't interfere with the operation of the business establishment. When picketing is done legally and properly, the results can be extremely gratifying.

22 Moving On

The effect described in the previous chapter was caused by making the alternative to settlement too costly. By raising or escalating the cost, the company was pressured to deal with a problem it preferred to ignore. As the pressure mounted, the other side began to move toward a settlement of the dispute on acceptable terms. This escalation was caused by taking control of the situation away from the company and causing embarrassment and possible bad will among customers and potential customers. It was carried out within the law and with a demonstration of unswerving will and determination. It was also done in a way that brought it to the immediate attention of somebody who had the authority and good sense to stop it by satisfying the wronged customer.

Sometimes, escalation works more gradually, as in the
following situation that our family faced a few years ago,
and which I covered in more than 20 pages of detail in *How
I Turn Ordinary Complaints into Thousands of Dollars.* A
giant real estate company bought the building we were
living in and five other buildings on either side of it and
behind it. They planned to demolish the six houses and
build a huge high-rise.

As the buildings began to be vacated, by attrition and
settlement with the landlord, I was asked by one of the
principals how much it would take to get us to move out at
once. I suggested that the real estate company find us
another apartment to our liking, as they were well positioned to do, and pay our moving expenses and any
difference in the rent for a period of five years. There was
immediate agreement to this offer and I asked for a contract
to be sent us.

Later that day another principal called to say the first
principal had exceeded his authority in making our agreement. I was disappointed and pointed out that this sounded
like a standard technique used in bad faith negotiations.
The first deal is thrown out and its terms become a ceiling.
The next offer is then significantly lower. And so it went. I
agreed to the second, lesser offer. Amazingly, this offer was
also revoked and I was given a third, substantially lower,
offer and an ultimatum about accepting it ("or else").

I didn't like the third offer and considered the real
estate company's negotiating methods unconscionable but
our building was being vacated rapidly and four of the
other five buildings had been emptied and demolished. In
discussing the situation with my wife and daughter, I sensed
a slight uneasiness and we therefore decided to accept the
third offer.

When the contract arrived, however, it gave us only

about 90 percent of the little that had been promised. Our family considered the offer but this time I voiced my own feelings. I said that if the company had been honorable, even with the third offer, I would have signed the contract. But they'd reneged on three consecutive deals. Therefore, I wanted to reject their contract and be prepared to be the last tenant in the entire parcel. At that time we would either renegotiate the deal to our satisfaction, or, if they were able to dispossess us as they kept threatening they would, get nothing at all. I thought we had sufficient legal means of delaying the project, which I estimated at about a $10 million deal, and that they would prefer to meet our terms if we were able to cost them interest on their money and delay recoupment of their investment. The family took a deep breath and agreed.

I told the landlord we were rejecting the counteroffer and that they would have to come back to us last. When there were only three tenants still living in our building, we moved a piano into our apartment. I knew the relocator, whose office was in a vacated apartment on the ground floor, would soon report this fact to the landlord. That probably caused a few tightened stomach muscles. Shortly thereafter, the landlord called to reopen negotiations.

I asked for $25,000 net after taxes, an excellent apartment, which they'd found for us, moving and legal expenses, and some additional work done in the apartment: scraping and staining the floors, storm windows, painting, and a few other touches. I was told by one of the principals that Mr. Big (the principal principal) refused to accede to my demands. At that point I played my last card. I replied that while Mr. Big was reconsidering my offer, the price was going to rise $1,000 per calendar day. I said it was important to understand I meant calendar day and not business day as I didn't want any recriminations later.

In many negotiating situations it is important our time be given a value. While we may be willing to settle at a given price today, it should be pointed out to the other side that if the proposed settlement price is not accepted at once, the future settlement price will be higher. If this point is not made forcefully, the other side may think it has an open offer. The pressure is then shifted to us to lower our asking price when the other side rejects it. If we *raise* our price after it has been rejected, we maintain a strong bargaining position.

Several weeks later, they agreed to all of my original terms, if I dropped the thousand dollars per day penalty, which I was willing to do. I cautioned them about making certain the contract embodied our agreement correctly and completely, and gave them the name and address of an attorney to whom to send it. This time the contract was drafted without any mistakes and we all signed it.

The escalation was accomplished progressively. After they'd reneged on three deals, the first step was to inform them we would be the last tenants on the site. This set the tone for future negotiations. The next step was to move a piano into a 10-story apartment building slated for demolition and in which only three tenants still lived. Next, I was clear as to what we wanted when they finally asked and the price was high, more than deals one, two, and three combined. And finally when this offer was refused, I replied that the price was going up, not down. All of these escalations, I am convinced, plus the fact we were in a position to delay the project and probably cost them a few thousand dollars per day once we were the last tenants on the site, finally caused the other side to throw in the hand and deal again, this time off the top.

23 The Abominable Showman: "Gaslighting" Revisited

J. Guy Tally, an agent at one of the world's largest talent agencies, was notorious throughout the industry for not taking or returning calls. His unfailing disregard for the rights and feelings of others was directly responsible for a lengthening list of human misery that included scores of aborted careers, dozens of cases of elevated blood pressure, ulcers, melancholia, alcoholism, premature heart disease, a couple of suicides, and three other unnecessary deaths arising from a fatal automobile collision, which left the driver of the other vehicle and one of his passengers permanently injured. The amount of mental and emotional torment Tally had inflicted on his clients was off the deep end of the Richter scale.

His secretaries no longer found it necessary to use guile and penumbra in feinting callers into being kept waiting indefinitely on the line for Tally to pick up a telephone. Tally simply didn't take or return calls. A short man with a deep tan and ordinary features, he took exquisite care of himself. His moustache and thinning hair were kept carefully trimmed and he was expensively turned out. Manicured and sleek, his country club and men's salon bills (which were carelessly paid every few months) would have supported a small nursing home.

And Guy liked to keep people waiting. On the rare occasions when a meeting was not scheduled on his own turf, he would arrive more than an hour late with smiling equanimity, unconcerned and unapologetic. His meetings, however, were almost always scheduled at his office and at his convenience. They were often suddenly changed or canceled abruptly by a secretary, without explanation. When a meeting was actually confirmed and reconfirmed by the anxious invitees, it was a common sight at the agency to watch the small cluster of talent and their advisors congregate in the reception area at the appointed time.

As time passed without sign or sight of Tally, the small, increasingly anxious group was reduced from good-natured badinage to terse requests for more coffee. One by one they finally stopped pretending not to notice they were being treated as nonpersons and they began to lose face among themselves. In deference to the putative importance of the guests, the receptionist would offer them the good china in lieu of cardboard cups but such a small impersonal gesture in no way made up for Tally's lack of decency. Of such bits and pieces as the fact that Tally happened to be in a position to undertake important career moves for a client was his power fashioned.

By the time Guy finished admonishing his cleaning woman and handling other pressing business on the telephone and had instructed one of his secretaries to shepherd the group into his office, they were strung taut and edgy and the dregs of the coffee urn were churning in their innards.

Tally's reputation and modus operandi came to the attention of Chad Wainwright, who had recently returned to the States after a stint in the Peace Corps, and who was working in the talent agency's mailroom that summer. Chad and Guy were about the same age but Chad had seen a great deal more of the world at ground level and his perspective of Guy was clear and undistorted. He was also in the snug position of wanting nothing whatever from Guy.

After hearing about Tally for several weeks Chad did some firsthand information gathering unobtrusively in his daily rounds of delivering the mail. He was soon convinced. Talent, always in short supply, was being nudged toward the endangered species list by this abominable showman. Chad decided to intervene.

He enlisted the help of an English friend he'd met in Chelsea. Charlotte, whose diction was faultless Upper, called Tally's office and asked to speak with him, As expected, her name was added to the list of those whose calls would never be returned. After a decent interval Charlotte called again, this time at 1:15 P.M., a time Tally was sure to be enjoying one of his lavish lunches at the agency's expense. She imparted to Tally's secretary that

110

Tally had been named as one of the principal legatees of a rather sizeable estate. For verisimilitude, the name of the decedent had been selected from the obituary page of a recent weekly *Variety*. Mr. Thatcher, the executor of the estate and her employer, wished to have Mr. Tally return the call at his earliest convenience. Mr. Thatcher's number? Oh, yes, he'd be in New York at TE8-9970 until 4 P.M.

When Tally returned from lunch shortly after three, Mr. Thatcher's was the only call that was returned. But the line was busy. And it was busy each time Tally's secretary tried for the next hour.

When Chad passed Tally's secretary's desk on his rounds near the close of business that day, he noticed on the outgoing calls sheet that a certain Mr. Thatcher had been called seven times. The rest of the page was blank. The fact that Guy Tally was having difficulty reaching "Thatcher's number" was no surprise to Chad, for any New York City telephone number ending with "9970" would produce a busy signal every time it was dialed.

A couple of days later, shortly after Tally left for one of his rare meetings out of the office, his secretary received a call. With typical British understatement, Charlotte explained that as Mr. Thatcher had not been responded to by Mr. Tally, despite two attempts, it was now a matter of some urgency they speak at once. Tally's secretary declared she'd tried to reach Mr. Thatcher at least half a dozen times but the line was always busy. Without commenting on the vain attempts, Charlotte stated that Mr. Thatcher was going to be back on the East Coast briefly. As time was now of the essence, Mr. Thatcher proposed they meet for breakfast at the restaurant in Newark Airport while Mr. Thatcher was between flights en route to Europe, at 7:45 A.M.

Sunday next. Could they get back, Tally's secretary inquired. No way, as Mr. Thatcher was already in the air.

Tally was put out of humor at the prospect of not only arising at dawn on a Sunday but of giving up a summer weekend as well. But principal legatees could make sacrifices and Tally was being shown to Mr. Thatcher's table at the appointed time and place.

At 8:15 that Sunday morning, Chad and Charlotte were awakened by the alarm clock they'd set the night before when they'd returned to a friend's beach house. The sun was up, bright and warming; it was a glorious day. Charlotte instructed the man who answered the telephone to tell Mr. Tally his party'd been slightly delayed.

Tally grumpily ordered breakfast. Along about Tally's third cup of coffee, "Mr. Thatcher" conveyed his regrets, without explanation. On the way home in the taxi it was clear to Tally that "Thatcher" was a deliberate fiction and his legacy (which he'd mentioned in confidence to a couple of intimates and which was being bruited about the agency mailroom the same day) was nonexistent. But who—and why?

On Monday Tally's first office-mail delivery was monumental. Every executive, in all of the agency's offices, foreign and domestic, had seemingly communicated with Tally. His name was officially hand-stamped on the inter-office envelopes. The messages were brief but disconcerting: "Punctuality is a virtue," "Time is money," "Courtesy saves but doesn't cost," "Arrogance is expendable."

Tally took his vacation earlier than he'd planned. He needed a rest, anyway. On unspoiled islands off the tourist routes, far from cities where *The Hollywood Reporter* and *Variety* were sold, he began to unwind. He discovered that people didn't have to be flogged to be helpful and that human motivation had a broader fame than career advancement.

He returned, refreshed and relaxed, and is now a successful personal manager of a few carefully chosen clients. Chad Wainwright is a junior agent, said by everybody to be a real comer.

24 The Home Court Advantage

Sports fans have long been aware of the phenomenon known as the home court advantage. Year after year professional, semi-professional, college, and amateur teams in all sports consistently win a greater proportion of their home games than games played away from home. Good, bad or mediocre, a team will do better at home than it will on the road.

Probably the most striking demonstration of home court advantage occurs in professional basketball. The Boston Celtics may beat the New York Knicks by a wide margin at home, only to lose to them, often by an equally lopsided score, a day or two later in New York. What is the explanation for this and how may we obtain this important bonus for ourselves in our daily lives?

The most important factor involves the reactions of the spectators. Whereas courtrooms require stillness—an absence of spectator outburst—in order not to influence the thinking of jurors, a highly partisan, home-town crowd at a sports arena or a stadium is under no such stricture. The loud and clear rooting of fans operates on several levels; its effects are cumulative and often decisive. And while the specific patterns of fan encouragement have national and cultural variations, and differ for each sport, the general principles are always the same: to encourage the favored side and to discourage their opposition.

In professional basketball in the United States, for example, when the home team scores, crowd reaction is thunderously approving. But the home team need not score to merit approbation. If it prevents the opponents from scoring by stealing the ball or blocking a shot, or by some other alert defensive play, if it moves the ball well or threatens to score, approval from the fans is immediately forthcoming. At other times encouragement will be in the form of rhythmic applause that begins spontaneously in the stands and quickly spreads and intensifies.

On the other hand, a score registered by the visitors is greeted with stony silence or disapproval, and their deft defensive play gets no encouragement whatever from the crowd. But their misplays, particularly in crucial situations, will usually be cheered. The effect in boosting home-team morale and demoralizing the opposition is thus double-edged.

The home court advantage also operates off the playing field. Businessmen, for example, often vie with one another to schedule important meetings at their own offices. On their own "home court" they are more confident and in better control of the variables. Telephone calls and other distractions can be eliminated (or deliberately introduced). Visitors may sometimes have calls transferred to the meeting, but more than one or two such nonemergency interruptions is considered rude or out of place and therefore counterproductive. The chief effect is psychological; the visitor has had to come calling and it is he who is typically at a disadvantage.

A similar gain may be scored by choosing the restaurant for a luncheon or dinner meeting. While you are repeatedly and respectfully deferred to by your last name and the captain and his staff hover solicitously nearby, alive to your every wish, the person with whom you are meeting may soon feel uncared for, rejected, left out, one down.

The home court advantage need not be limited to the actual home court; it can be transported. During wartime, for example, the entertainment of our troops stationed thousands of miles from home, particularly by talent with whom they were familiar in civilian life, invariably had pronounced morale-building effects.

Wouldn't it be a desirable bonus if we could not only give ourselves this advantage but take it with us wherever we went? We can and it is easier than it appears. Here are some mental sets that have worked for me:

First, get yourself *up*. Be your own biggest fan, not by cheering yourself loudly, but by doing it *silently*. Do it mentally, by acts of will, not by speech. Regardless of how you feel about yourself, or how others may describe you, think of something that made you feel good about yourself. It doesn't matter what it is, so long as it makes you feel positive toward yourself. Reach back as far into the past as you like. Remember when you learned to read, to write, to speak, to walk? The harder it is for you to think of other examples, the more necessary it is to do so.

Without discussing these examples with anybody, think about them as often as you like (the more often the better). Let them fill your mind. It will help you feel more like somebody who *deserves* to have his or her own personal cheerleader. You can magnify the salubrious effect by adding other mental cheerleaders. Become familiar with this good feeling about yourself and carry it with you as your own personal talisman. And, of course, stop hurting and punishing yourself by dwelling on past failures and missed opportunities, and on how others deprived you of a better life. Silently cheer when you do well but refuse to replay in your mind anything negative.

The final step in the process of creating the home court advantage is to surround yourself with people whose attitudes are positive and to avoid the naysayers, those who seem always to be unsupportive, even antagonistic, toward you. If you were sitting in a football stadium, surrounded by people rooting against your team, wouldn't you change your seat? Wouldn't you enjoy the game more if you walked across the stands and joined those rooting for your team?

This is not to suggest associating only with like-minded people. Not at all. But if people are negative toward you, it is a needless drain on your time, energies, and emotions. There is nothing to be gained by allowing yourself to be put in the position of having constantly to justify or defend yourself. And this kind of negative feedback tends to destroy enthusiasm. It keeps us anchored in troubled waters and utterly limits our potential. Sidestep these people and use your energies constructively and creatively. Let them find another target while you go about building your life. It

117

is not status but attitude which is important in this context. Seek those whose attitudes are constructive and optimistic, and avoid those who habitually negate life, regardless of station or status. This approach will leave you free to grow toward the possible instead of tethered, immobilized into atrophy and decay.

25 Results with a Snap: The One Picture That's Really Worth a Thousand Words

In the Middle Ages people were extremely reluctant to give their names to strangers. It was generally believed that anybody who knew their names could somehow exercise control over them. Nowadays many of the people we deal with seem to place much credence in this venerable belief and cling to anonymity. Ma Bell's people often choose not to yield up even their identifying numbers, which have always been poor substitutes for more traditional nomenclature. Isn't it foolish to insist it was operator 349 who insulted us when it might have been number 345? And there are so many different company offices and the turnover is so great, how can we be sure?

While the control which a name gives us is slippery at best, it does provide a starting point in redressing the excesses of the marketplace. It is certainly preferable to know that Mr. Tschegorian removed the television set from the den than that it was "a man in a green Mackinaw." But unless the person is wearing a name tag or identifying badge and the transaction is face to face, we must be sure to request the name at the outset, before the slightest hint of trouble. And our voice must resonate with good will and benevolence lest we seem to be trying to wrest control.

"How do you do." (Make this a declaration not a question, for one question too many may make the other person bristle with suspicion.) "My name is _____. May I ask what is yours?" (Your most gracious and innocent smile will help supply the proper voice tone here.)

If we defer the introductions, arrogant and/or intransigent personnel are likely to ignore our request to identify themselves or deliberately give us a false name. And we are all the more likely to be abruptly disconnected on telephones when our request is made after an impasse is reached and it is clear we don't intend to let the matter rest there.

There are companies whose employees routinely hand out fictitious names to their customers. An entire department may be assigned the same fictitious name so that we have no way of knowing that the person we are speaking with on the second or third occasion is not the same one we spoke with originally. The fact that the second or third person has no idea what we're talking about is artfully disguised to pass as ordinary incompetence. And this deceitful, slipshod way of dealing with us has been deliberately and methodically built into the system. It's not simply an occasional malfunction of the system with which we must contend; it's part of the method and therefore designed to produce malfunctions regularly.

Some companies give their personnel names that attempt to identify not them but *us!* The first name is one that has no gender; it may belong to a man or a woman: Shaw, Adrian, Crawford. Or they may use a first initial in lieu of a name. This allows *anybody* to pretend he or she is the person we called. If we are having a problem with a department store bill, we may be given (as the name of somebody who will help us with the problem) a name which identifies us as somebody who is suspected of having too many problems with bills or an unjustified problem with this particular bill, or even an objectionable tone of voice in discussing a bill.

People who allegedly don't pay bills promptly; those who would like to be credited for a payment made by check that has been paid by their bank but not properly credited by the store; others who'd like to correct an error on a bill and whose letters have been ignored; all of these and others are lumped together and labeled in a way that indicates that those tagged are "bill problems." These decisions, of course, are always reasonable as they have been made after a few seconds of thought by somebody we were fooled into believing was finally going to deal with the matter at hand, only to find we were again going to be shuttled to the next person in the inefficient and poorly designed process.

One of the major credit card companies has refined the process of dispersing responsibility even further. They don't use fictitious names and they take great exception if they are so accused. What they don't tell us is that they use real names of actual people but the people don't work for the company as claimed. This major service company has simply provided another service for its customers. They

121

have rented or purchased the right to use other people's names. Typically, these names are given to us with a first initial but no first name and the surnames are usually common and easy to pronounce: Brown, Green, Jones. We are told, usually by mail, that the individual named is our "personal representative" and is to be contacted in the unlikely event any problem arises. I sometimes wonder what would happen if credit-card holders somehow were able to unearth the real people allegedly behind these names and began to contact them.

My "personal representative" used to be located in New York City, where I live. Presumably for my convenience, my "personal representative" using the real name (not fictitious) of somebody else is now located in Miami where he or she (the first initial has no gender so anybody can claim it) refuses to accept collect calls. I use the company's New York tieline number to Miami when I call and recommend this method as preferable to paying for unnecessary toll calls. In addition, the toll-free information operator (800-555-1212) may be able to supply many other long distance numbers which will entail no cost. (Although the telephone company does not make a directory of toll-free numbers available to its subscribers, such directories are available in paperback books.)

But names, helpful as they may be, are fallible. I've therefore put a slight twist on in-person confrontations with indifference, recalcitrance, arrogance, and rudeness in ordinary commercial dealings. Let's say we've been mistreated or ignored at a department store or the person to whom we've gone for help with a store problem is more interested in his or her personal conversation than in solving the problem. Consider the effect of casually taking out an instant camera and snapping the photograph of the wrongdoer. For some elusive reason that may have some connection with the importance attached to withholding names in the Middle Ages, that person doesn't want us to have his or her photograph. It causes the person to become extremely attentive and curious and we will probably be asked for an explanation. When we reply that we wanted to have documentary evidence to submit to Mr. Big as to why we no longer deal with the store, it is usually a short step to trading the photo for a quick result.

There are lots of other applications that are a snap. For example, how would a typical restaurateur feel if an unhappy diner summoned him to the table to show him a photograph of a terrible meal he'd just been served? Wouldn't he make an effort to please the diner and retrieve the snapshot? Or, a repair person tells us the item to be repaired (television set, stereo component, washing machine, etc.) has to go into the shop and he doesn't know when it'll be ready nor how much it will cost—at which point you frame him, focus, and snap. The surprise alone can restructure the situation so that our rights stop being trampled, and its effectiveness is roughly proportional to the reliability of the company on the other side of the transaction. But taken judiciously, one photograph may indeed be more eloquent than a lot of verbiage.

26 Sound Decisions

George W., an assistant buyer for a large department store, lived in a studio apartment in a renovated building not far from the store. One day, a couple moved in above him. During the ensuing couple of weeks George was unable to get even a modest night's sleep, and of the psyche-restoring, dreamy, REM sleep vital to mental health, he was completely deprived. He kept hoping his punishment would soon end, for how many ways could two people rearrange their furniture in a studio apartment, and how many custom-made bookshelves would they be required to saw and hammer in the wee hours, if their appearances were not completely deceptive?

At length, the interior decorating and the carpentry were completed and he looked forward to the speedy restoration of his health and spirits. But this expectation was short-lived. Although he wasn't due at the store until 9:45, George was awakening, regularly and unaccountably, at 6:23. And he was one of those people for whom the sounds of city traffic and of the successive alarm clocks of his earlier-rising neighbors were enough to prevent further sleep. He soon realized, by the precision with which he was arising, that a neighbor's alarm clock was responsible. But whose?

Although he knew in his heart where the cause lay, he was not one to act without sufficient evidence. After all, renovated buildings are rather flimsy constructions, and sound, as he had learned in high-school physics, travels mysteriously. He set his alarm clock for 6:15 the following morning, voluntarily giving up a few minutes of sorely needed sleep in order to be alert at 6:23. Once he determined which of his neighbors housed the offending signal, he would surely be able to work out a mutually satisfactory arrangement.

The next morning as George had suspected, it was the new upstairs neighbors' clock that had been set at 6:23. He waited for a neutral time to call, like 8:45 P.M.

"Hi, I'm George W. I live in the apartment below yours. Welcome to the building. Now that you've had a chance to get set up, I wonder whether we could try to work out a better place to keep your alarm clock."

"Hold it," George was instructed. "I think I'd better put my husband on."

George patiently explained to the man that the problem was created not by the fact that the alarm was set for 6:23 but by the clock's placement on the floor. Had to do with the way sound traveled. The man, who had come across strangers before, agreed to find a different site for the clock and the situation seemed remedied—until George began to be awakened regularly at 6:38, give or take a couple of minutes.

He soon discovered the source of the latest disturbance and attempted to impart this information to his upstairs neighbors, this time in person.

"I want to thank you very much for moving the clock," George told the man who opened the door for him, after he identified himself.

"That's all right. No trouble at all."

"That was very kind of you but there's still one thing standing between me and a night's sleep."

"What's that?" asked the man, the smile on his face giving way to a scowl.

"Impact noise," said George evenly.

"What?"

"You have a convertible bed or a high riser, am I right?"

"What about it?" said the man. His tone had suddenly become hostile.

"It's just that when you reconvert to a sofa or a daybed or whatever, there's that last jolting noise when it snaps into position at 6:38 every morning."

"What's your point?" the upstairs neighbor inquired sullenly.

"Impact noise," said George sweetly. "The worst kind. It's like the situation with the alarm clock. If you were to hang the alarm clock from a light cord, it probably wouldn't wake anybody up. But if you place it on the floor or against a wall it would, because there's direct contact with a sound-conducting surface."

"Hang my alarm clock from a light cord? What the hell are you talking about?"

"It has nothing to do with your alarm clock. It's hypothetical. Maybe I picked a bad example," George conceded. "Let me put it this way: *hypothetically*, if you were to bang two sticks together in your apartment, the noise produced probably wouldn't disturb anybody. But if you banged the sticks against one of the walls or the floor or the ceiling, it *would* bother other people even though the actual noise level remained the same. See what I mean?"

"Listen," said the man, stretching his body to its full height, "we went along with the alarm clock. What the hell do you want now!"

"I'd really appreciate it if you could leave your bed open until later in the morning. Maybe until nine o'clock. Or, if that's not convenient, maybe until you get home from work. It would make a lot of difference to my health."

"Look, are you nuts?" asked the neighbor. "We went along with the clock but now you're trying to run our lives."

"Not exactly," demurred George downheartedly.

"Hey, forget it. Take a walk. Get lost!" replied the rangy owner of the convertible bed. Having discharged himself of those instructions, he abruptly ended the conversation by closing the door. George indistinctly heard him tell his wife something about hanging the alarm clock from a light cord, as he returned, defeated, to his apartment.

A colleague at the department store noticed George's drooped appearance, his chronic irritability and his increasing difficulty to last the course each day. She was kind and understanding and she offered a suggestion. By the time George arrived home that evening, his mental state had

127

undergone a complete transformation. Despite the chronic deprivation of sleep, he was exhilarated, for a pivotal decision had been made and the adrenalin was flowing. He was no longer simply going to absorb punishment. It was to be a battle for survival!

The first phase involved calling his neighbors twice in the early morning hours and hanging up. As his neighbors arose early, they probably retired early. Therefore, calls after midnight would probably awaken them. The plan called for them to receive the first call at about 2 A.M. This would awaken them and set them up for the second call, about three-quarters of an hour later, after they'd had an opportunity to get back to sleep. The second call would not only disturb their sleep but their nervous systems as well, for it would inform them that the former passive punching bag packed a sockdolager. Uncivilized? Perhaps. But this was war and George wasn't playing for a draw.

Once the the pattern was established, George would call before retiring each night and hang up immediately. He could then go to sleep confident that the neighbors would be expecting another call. Now and then he would make the second call to keep them off balance. As a precaution, George took his telephone off the hook before retiring. Phase one ended when the neighbors followed suit.

The second phase was primarily educational; the subject was impact noise. George would retire about eleven and set his alarm clock for 1:30, allowing time for a refreshing nap. Upon awakening he reached for a baseball bat, over one end of which he kept a pair of heavy tennis socks, in order to protect the fragile ceiling. He sharply thumped his ceiling once in the darkness. This would suddenly awaken the upstairs neighbors, who cursed the source of the disturbance without being aware of the method, for by the time they were fully aroused, all was quiet.

When they were disturbing George their greater number gave them an advantage. Now that the situation was reversed they were at a considerable disadvantage. Any noise either of them made in their apartment would keep both of them awake. And if either of them wanted to reciprocate against George when he or she awoke later in the morning, the other one would almost invariably be asleep.

As the weeks went by George was beginning to regain his health while his upstairs neighbors' were declining. The final phase, which was designed to evoke a bid for a truce, began when George, following his colleague's instructions to the letter, arrived home with the least expensive clarinet he could find in a pawnshop and a couple of reeds. After carefully boiling the mouthpiece, he was ready.

Before retiring, shortly before midnight, George stood atop his stove and aimed the clarinet toward the grate covering the exhaust duct, which served as an unacceptable substitute for windows in his studio apartment. Imperfectly covering the stops, George exuberantly produced a cacophony of squeaks and squeals sufficient to unnerve a battalion of Zen masters. He then took a relaxing warm shower, followed by another clarinet solo.

For two weeks his neighbors were thus assaulted twice each night.

On the fifteenth night, as George began his first selection, he thought he heard the sound of laughter issuing from the grate. When the laughter continued, George stopped playing and showered. As he began the second impromptu composition, he heard the unmistakable sound of a woman weeping. Although he stopped at once, the crying intensified and became hysterical.

Flooded with guilt and remorse, George realized he had been slavishly following his colleague's large-gauged instructions when expertise, specificity, delicacy, and precision were required. As the hysteria began to leave the human range, George ran to his telephone and dialed his upstairs neighbors. He had read of would-be suicides coaxed off narrow ledges by their ringing telephones. He expected the husband to answer, at which time he would contritely and unconditionally surrender. He kept dialing but the line was busy. Another pang of remorse and guilt stabbed him as he realized they were deliberately keeping their telephone off the hook as a defense against him.

Unwilling to commit himself too explicitly in writing but spurred to action, George typed a brief note stating that he hoped for a better relationship between them, and if there were anything he could do to improve it, he could be counted on. He quietly placed it under their door. They never replied. At the end of the month their apartment was vacant.

27 Yours for the Asking

The other day I read in one of the show business dailies that David Niven had given some annotated papers to the University of Wyoming. Questioned as to why the University of Wyoming, he was reported to have replied that they were the only ones who asked. This is a beautifully simple demonstration of the enormous power behind a request, any request.

Another example of asking for something is self-nomination, that is, asking for a promotion. This is a recognized way of advancing a career but I doubt that more than one person in a thousand plays this card even once in an entire career. I know a man who has used this technique in a whirlwind career that took him through more job titles in a Fortune 500 company than anybody else in its history. And when he'd gone as far and as fast as he could with that corporation, he moved over to a bank of career elevators that went even higher, with a giant conglomerate.

This man realized his career time was valuable. He refused to wait on the sidelines for promotions to seek him out. He took the initiative through self-nomination. When the situation developed to the point where a vertical move was possible, even if it meant creating a new position (which had the potential of being used as a springboard or catapult), this man constructed a well-reasoned memo to the executive who could institute the change of position for him. Sometimes the move was immediately initiated. Occasionally there was a slight delay. But always, merely asking created a preference in the mind of a sufficiently well-placed executive. When the time came, the self-nominator got the promotion. After all, nobody else had asked.

Asking has many other useful applications. In litigations, for example, the plaintiff's brief contains a section known as the "prayer for relief." This is only a formal way of asking for what the plaintiff wants. Advertisers ask us to behave in ways desirable to them all the time: "Send in right away." "Buy it." "Try it." "Get it." "Mail this coupon in today." "Cut coupon along dotted line." Etc. Salespeople are taught to "ask for the order." The reason advertisers and salespeople ask for our business is they know asking increases sales.

We hear about the "list of demands" in union/management negotiations. Again, this list is only a means of asking for what is wanted. It wouldn't make much sense to walk into a negotiating session without knowing what we want but otherwise sensible people do it regularly in their daily lives. I found, in dealing with purveyors of bad goods and terrible services, that somewhere near the end of the negotiation, the other side almost invariably asked "What do you want?" If I didn't have a clear idea of what to ask for, how could I expect to get it?

Who knows better than we what we want? And what do we risk by asking, as weighed against the potential gain? Why simply accept the apparent limitations of a given situation without inquiry as to how it might be made better? I was recently audited by the Internal Revenue Service. I met with the examiner in a large room, the temperature of which was at least eighty-five degrees. It was oppressively hot and uncomfortable. When I asked the examiner whether she would mind if I removed my jacket and opened my tie, and whether she were uncomfortable, she replied that she knew it was bad for her health to work in that heat, and extremely uncomfortable, but there was nothing that could be done about it. What had been done? Nothing, beyond an occasional mild complaint to the maintenance people. I assured her and some of the other examiners who joined the conversation that I could have the room at a comfortable temperature within a day. When I finished my list of possible solutions, they approved of one call to the Department of Health. When that call wasn't answered by anybody (it was made during a lunch hour) they asked me to desist, as they were fearful of the possible consequences to them. A couple of timid attempts, and they all accepted that set of givens as immutable when it could have been changed easily.

Suppose we go to a restaurant and peruse the menu. None of the items particularly appeals to us but we make our selections from the menu without attempting to change

133

a comma. What do we risk by asking whether there is anything available *not* on the menu? If this is done in a polite and friendly way, without denigrating the hospitality of the establishment, we may be delightfully surprised with the results.

What is infinitely worse than accepting the apparent limitations of a menu is accepting the apparent limitations of a status quo in our lives that is joyless, insipid, unsatisfying. The starting point in improving situations must be ourself. We should begin to ask ourselves what we want, specifically and concretely, before we can ask others. Vague feelings won't do nor will an abstraction or something amorphous that cannot be touched and grasped. Abstractions are hard to come by in reasonable lengths of time without magic wands. Concrete realities can be ours through our own efforts; once we have been specific, we have an objective toward which to move.

Some people may consider asking for something too forward or demanding. Perhaps, but there are tactful ways of asking. "Would it be possible?" is one such way of taking the sting out of requesting something to which we are entitled, without making the other person feel subservient or put upon. I've received many letters from people who asked for help with a situation or problem in a straightforward manner. If I thought I had some ideas which might work, I sent them along. If not, I told them so, but I answered every letter. On a couple of occasions I've sought advice or information from strangers who were kind enough to give me the benefit of their knowledge and experience. My responses and theirs were received simply by asking.

Some may think of asking as a selfish act. It needn't be. Completely cooperative relationships may begin with a request. When I asked my publisher for a contract on this book and sent a few pages to indicate what I had in mind, I sought a joint venture in which both of us would benefit.

Mutuality and cooperation are also inherent in marriage and applying for a job but they both ordinarily require asking. In many other situations, like the restaurant which has food available which happens not to be printed on the menu, our gain is not at anyone's expense. If we are pleased with the meal, both we and they gain, yet the reluctance to ask is pervasive.

When my daughter was going to college out of town, she sometimes took a bus back to school, which required a change to another bus about twenty miles from the college. I learned that when the first bus was late, the second bus left at the scheduled time and my daughter and others had to wait several hours for the next bus. I subsequently called the dispatcher of the first bus company and asked whether he could request the second bus to wait. He was happy to do so and the problem was solved. What impressed me most was that nobody else had asked.

The loose-fitting steamhole lid I described in the chapter "Keeping the Lid On" probably disturbed a thousand families every night, but mine was the only request for a remedy. If we want help, shouldn't we ask for it?

28 We Are Not Alone

Most disagreements between buyers and sellers can easily be resolved by the parties involved. A little skill in presenting and pressing justified complaints; the determination not to be ravaged in the marketplace; and the tenacity and perseverance that won't permit our rights to be trampled, ignored, or shunted aside, will have almost any dispute involving goods and services by the heels before too long. However, sometimes a particular merchant, professional, service person, or other seller of bad goods or terrible services may wish to take more from us than is warranted, or give us less, and then to write us off as customers or clients, taking the attitude that if we are displeased, we may sue him. On the rarest of occasions, of course, litigation may be the appropriate recourse. But courts and lawyers are usually prohibitively time-consuming and expensive. Therefore, when our own best efforts at redress seem unavailing, before considering legal action, we should try to discover what other forums are available in which to seek our remedy. This knowledge can bring us the relief that has eluded us, often without even putting us to the necessity of formally seeking such outside help.

There is a wide assortment of federal, state, and local regulatory agencies and other bodies, public and private, which regulate various industries, professions, trades, and other business organizations. Although I prefer to handle my own consumer complaints without outside help, I have on occasion resorted to this free help, to excellent effect. These mechanisms place themselves between us and the sellers. They are not all equally effective but their intervention, which can be set in motion with a telephone call, followed by a letter, can have a civilizing effect on would-be predators in the marketplace. Even more satisfying are situations in which a proper reference to the specific breach of the rules under which a particular agency or other authoritative body would intervene, causes a truculent miscreant to abruptly fold the hand, removing the necessity to invoke the outside help. After all, isn't it preferable to make good the transaction with me than to become embroiled in a losing battle with a regulatory agency?

For example, I once took a telephone-answering machine to a large multinational company for repairs, as recommended by the machine's manufacturer. I was told I'd be called when the cause of the problem was located, at which time we'd discuss the charges for repairing the machine. The company also said there was a specified minimum charge for examining the machine. A few days later I received a bill and a written notice to pick up the repaired machine. The "balance due" was several times the minimum charge and included an item for new batteries.

When I arrived I asked for my old batteries, explaining that I preferred that brand and type of battery, and told the man in possession of my machine that my batteries had tested in excellent working order the day before I'd brought in the machine. My batteries were not forthcoming. I explained that under the Department of Consumer Affairs regulations, anything replaced during repairs had to be returned to the customer and if the charges were not agreed upon or considerably exceeded the minimum charge, the customer had to be given an opportunity to decide not to pay them. The man snarlingly informed me (I believe he was trying to intimidate me, although he may have had a speech defect) that if I didn't pay the bill, they would keep the machine.

After I paid the bill and made sure the machine was operating properly, I called the management of the company at its corporate headquarters, outlined the situation, and soon received a letter of apology and full reimbursement plus "appreciation for bringing the matter to our attention." With regard to their "not adhering to the Consumer Protection laws of the City of New York, our consumer relations people, at my request, are checking into the matter. If, in fact, we presently are not adhering to these laws, we will make immediate changes to conform to them, this I assure you."

A number of cities have a Department of Consumer Affairs. As the name implies, they are oriented toward helping consumers. Their regulations have the force of law in protecting us. Their employees will provide printed copies of their regulations and if a particular problem lies outside their jurisdiction, they are likely to be able to refer us to the proper agency. For example, if our complaint involved a short-weighted package, we might be referred to the Department of Marketing. I have always found the New York City Department of Consumer Affairs helpful and ready to act promptly if a matter involved an alleged breach of its regulations. This kind of protection is important because it covers small matters that could not otherwise be handled without expertise and/or prohibitive outlays of time and effort. Consumer Affairs regulations discipline the marketplace for all of us.

In one instance, I ordered broiled beef as an entree at a sushi restaurant and received some heavily charcoaled food. I asked the server for a substitute dish, explaining that I try to avoid charcoaled food, which I believe to be carcinogenic, and that the menu had led me astray by listing the item as broiled, not charcoal broiled. The manager soon appeared and insisted the dish was not charcoal-broiled despite the large amounts of charcoal on it. There was no pretense of politeness in the other side's presentation. Although I didn't eat the food, the restaurant's employees insisted I pay for it, which I did by signing for it on a credit card.

At a convenient time, I called the Department of Consumer Affairs and followed with a letter. They soon sent an inspector to investigate. Although the restaurant wasn't fined (their plea of ignorance was accepted), they were instructed to change their menus to conform to the facts and were ordered to return the price of the entree to me, which they did.

On another occasion, I arose shortly after dawn, missed

139

breakfast, and took an early flight to an out-of-town meeting. Returning home on a late afternoon flight the same day, I had no sooner stretched out in my seat and fallen asleep, than I was kicked awake by somebody behind me. A very young child seemed to be kicking the back of my seat at random. I looked to the woman accompanying the child for relief but was ignored. After several additional kicks, I suggested that perhaps the woman and the child might exchange seats so I could get some sleep. I was glared at for this suggestion but no further notice of me was taken. I asked the flight attendant what could be done and suggested that children under a certain age were not entitled to occupy seats alone under Federal Aviation Authority (FAA) rules. It's not easy to be the apparent adversary of a child and I suppose I was considered the heavy; nothing was done. I then suggested that it might be possible for me to change my seat but was told there were no empty seats on the flight and indeed I didn't see any. Shortly after we began our descent pattern, I was told somebody was willing to exchange seats with me and I was led to a seat which turned out to be in the smoking section. As we were about to land, I kept this seat despite the discomfitingly poor quality of the air.

The bottom line was that after I was able to quote a passage from an FAA booklet to the effect that children under the age of two had to share a seat with an adult, I was offered, and accepted, full reimbursement for that flight. Up to that point, however, the airline management expressed great sorrow at my discomfiture and were certain future flights would be wonderful. There simply was nothing more they could do.

Sellers sometimes refuse to play by the rules even when they are clearly set forth. Under the New York City rent-control law, for example, landlords are required to paint an apartment every three years. When our apartment was due to be painted, I called the agent and gave him our choice of colors. One delay after another ensued. As we were not looking forward to the inconvenience of painting, I didn't press the landlord although I did call the agent from time to time.

When almost two years had elapsed with no sign of the painters, I told the agent we intended to make a formal request through the Department of Housing and Buildings, which we did. The order was duly received by the landlord and a painter finally arrived. We requested the same shade of white as had previously been used to paint our apartment; the painter agreed. We prepared the premises for painting and the painter kept the appointment. However, he began to paint a grayish white, not the white we'd specified. When we called this to his attention, he pretended not to understand us and then told us there was no way to give us the white we wanted in only one coat of paint and we were entitled to only one coat. Displeased with the delay and duplicity, I asked him to leave at once, which he did.

Within two days I had an inspector determine that the grayish color was not the original white, to which we were entitled. The landlord was ordered to paint the premises in its original color on penalty of reducing the rent if the order were not complied with within a few days. The agent called me (a first) and agreed to order the paint we specified (including the brand name) as well as supply a different, extremely competent painter, who completed the job without further delay. Without help from a government agency this could not have been accomplished so expeditiously, if at all.

Unfortunately, many people allow their rights to be trampled simply because they are unaware of how easy it is to ascertain these rights and then to have them enforced. If the source of help isn't immediately clear and there is no friend who knows and no consumer affairs department to ask for a referral, your congressman or a local librarian can be of enormous help. If more people learned to assert their rights appropriately, the sellers of goods and services would become more responsive and responsible.

29   Too Much Dictation

Dictatorial bosses present special problems. Subordinates are ordinarily in an exceedingly weak position to get the upper hand on immediate supervisors who trample their rights and feelings, sometimes flying into rages if their rigid, unreasonable demands are not acceded to at once. Often those who mete out such Draconian treatment are merely following a script written and orchestrated by oversubmissive parents. Sometimes such an unfeeling person may be the victim of a superior like himself—the battered underling becoming the battering boss. But such psychologizing won't heal the damaging wounds tyrannical executives continually inflict on those unfortunate enough to report to them, or provide the antidote for the many needless poisonings of the latters' spirits.

Of course, these cruel individuals are not all bad. They may be quite insensitive to the deaths of ten thousand innocent earthquake victims in Paraguay but moved to tears by the televised plight of a stray cat. Encouraging these human sentiments and, wherever possible, placing reasonable limitations on such a supervisor's wanton disregard of the dignity of others cannot fail to have a salubrious effect. Loyal subordinates should therefore regard such undertakings as obligatory. If they also, incidentally, provide relief for the subordinate, who would object? A frontal assault on the boss's daemons would be presumptuous, but a more subtle, oblique approach may bestow the same healthful benefits at a much more acceptable risk.

In the following illustrative example, the long-suffering underling is nattering on the telephone with a friend, behind the closed door of his cubicle. Noticing the closed door, the boss seizes an opportunity to reinforce the pecking order. Deliberately slamming his flat palm against the door as noisily as possible and crashing it open so that it flies back against the wall, boss startlingly and discourteously invades the privacy of the underling's sanctum. Boss follows this salvo by walking about underling's desk and up against his chair, intimidating him further by encroaching on his territory.

Boss is confident underling, as usual, will timidly inform the party at the other end of the line that he will have to get back to him later, and hang up. This time, however, underling detects an opportunity to improve boss's mental health and dutifully responds. Keeping his wits about him,

144

underling speaks into his telephone while boss breathes down his neck.

"Yes, Gladys. I've made all the arrangements for Aunt Margaret's funeral. We'll have 15 limousines at the chapel. (Big sigh.) I've already taken care of that . . . The insurance will probably cover it but in the meantime I'll lay out whatever is necessary. Who cares about money at a time like this?"

This should be enough to cause the boss to slink out of underling's cubicle, perhaps quietly signalling that he'll speak with underling later, at a more opportune time. When they meet later, the boss may offer his and/or the firm's heartfelt condolences, while underling nods silently.

"Thank you, J.R. I'm afraid I'm going to have to be away from my desk for a few days."

"Of course. Naturally. We understand. Take all the time you need."

This simple illustration combines three elements which are sure-fire if mixed with a little care. First, there is the pattern-breaking behavior by which underling disappointed the boss's expectations in the course of the latter's encroachment. Instead of the accustomed full retreat, underling held his ground by remaining on the telephone. Acting contrary to a well-established behavior pattern is always disorienting, like the effect of looking through the wrong end of a telescope or wandering into the fun house of an amusement park.

Immediately pressing this advantage, so that boss had no time to insist on his prerogatives, underling presented the overbearing superior with a new and unexpected frame of reference; instead of overhearing banter or gossip, the boss was made privy to a personal tragedy with which he could identify. Everybody is uneasily aware of his own mortality. Successfully tested variations include initial notices of incurable diseases, untimely deaths (at ages under forty), complete mental breakdowns of loved ones, and the new stations in life as domestics or salesclerks of internationally acclaimed movie stars of a bygone era. Immediate family members are never named as victims, finessing baskets of fruit and embarrassing messages of condolences. Thus, the second element is to put into proper perspective the boss's mean-minded attempt to exact some trivial sign of his own importance as compared with matters of vastly greater significance: irreversible losses among relatives, close friends or celebrities, which involve life, liberty, property, reputation or health, all of which suggest human vulnerability and uncertainty and are chosen for the purpose of making the boss suddenly and uncomfortably aware of his own defenselessness.

Third, there is the injection of a healthy dose of guilt. The boss, frozen in the moment of trying to heap some wretchedly petty abuse on an innocent object, has glimpsed a personal tragedy with heavy identification. Much cause for guilt, and since it is all implicit, indirect, unspoken, the boss can only internalize it and reproach himself.

As a bonus, the intended victim rewards himself with a few days away from the office, thoughtfully bestowing another kindness on the boss, who earlier has had a hygienic limit placed upon his excessive behavior and who now, by virtue of his belated display of concern and understanding, is mercifully released from guilt and self-reproach.

30 How to Control Time

One evening while my wife was preparing dinner, she asked whether I'd mind buying a couple of pounds of onions. The round trip to the market, only two blocks away, took a pressure-elevating three-quarters of an hour. First, the elevator operator of our apartment building had to be coaxed from his television program in the basement. Ringing several times to summon the elevator is considered bad form by my neighbors. And the staff has made it clear they resent being disturbed by even a second ring except during commercials or within three weeks of Christmas. As I was unaware of the commercial formatting of the particular program the man "on duty" happened to be watching, the enforced wait soon had my pulse racing. The distance to the market was easily traversed although the icy sidewalks, carelessly unswept, might have presented obstacles to one less nimble.

With some help I found the onions tucked away with the produce. Here I had a choice: to save time by getting the prepackaged and already priced but containing some onions in each package the other shoppers had wisely rejected; or to select a few attractive onions, find the produce person and wait for him to weigh and bag them and mark their price with a black crayon. I chose the crayon.

The "express" checkout line, reserved for those with no more than six items, included several shoppers whose carts were piled to the gunwales. As I was not especially pressed, I chose one of the nonexpress lines without complaint, although I was curious, in passing, whether six separate cans of the same item would be deemed six items or considered as a six-pack. I wondered who was empowered to make that ruling and whether it would have made a difference if the six cans were individually priced or were six for a specified sum.

I had more than enough time to consider these questions as several people before me paid by check and each check required the approval of an employee who had to be found in a different hiding place each time. The person who was bagging and boxing the orders on our checkout line must have grown bored for he left to wander down one of the aisles and I never saw him again. This was a loss as the "express" line, whose lack of a bag-and-box person I had factored into my choice of the nonexpress line, was at the point where my turn would have been next.

As I placed the onions on the conveyor belt, the checker

dropped a large bottle of soda that had been bought by the woman before me. It burst on impact and the line halted while the checker called for a mop. Checkers, I have tentatively concluded from admittedly insufficient observation, either have no opposable thumb or five of them on each hand. There was a sudden shortage of bags small enough for the onions but after a thorough search a stack of suitable-size bags was located and I was soon retracing my steps across the ice. After a short wait for a station break I was whisked back to home and hearth.

Three-quarters of an hour for 57¢ worth of onions! And, of course, I wasn't alone. Millions of people waste billions of hours each year. To suggest that much valuable time is wasted is not intended to champion the so-called Protestant work ethic; it has nothing to do with whether or not the Devil finds work for idle hands. Personally, I value fun and recreation and a number of other uses to which time may be put. It is the time needlessly and habitually wasted, the time over which we do not exercise choices, to which I am referring—the blocks of time we allow ourselves and others to siphon out of our lives, often without full awareness that we are giving up one of our most valuable assets, an unduplicatable one that can never be regained. And when we are actively engaged in wasting time each day we have less opportunity to pause and discover what we would like to be doing.

There is no meaningful way to get the upper hand in our lives without controlling our expenditures of time. We may occasionally deal with inconsiderate people who are able to inconvenience us now and then by failing to keep appointments, by engaging us in extended conversations in person or on the telephone, or by a number of dawdling inefficiencies. But in examining the phenomenon of time-wasting, we are looking for the most part at self-inflicted wounds. In the average home in the United States, about 44 hours per week are spent by viewers staring passively at a television screen, watching programs they didn't really want to see.

The first step in getting the upper hand on wasted time is to plug the leaks on the two or three major drains, those areas that don't provide a fair return on our time. These will usually be unrewarding activities done by rote or habit. Television viewing is one obvious example. If people consciously selected the programs they watched and really enjoyed them, this might be an acceptable way of spending time. But unlike movie-going, which involves a conscious choice of which film to see, television viewers don't watch programs, they watch television, continually tuning in and out, and eating, drinking, telephoning, reading, etc., while they change channels, hoping to find something that will engage their diminished spans of attention. If some of this viewing time between dinner and retiring were spent otherwise, the rewards could be substantial. This period may be viewed as an asset we can learn to treasure and enjoy.

We will be able to carve out the most useful blocks of time from our principal time killers. Some people waste hours on the telephone; others do chores, like shopping for onions, banking or buying postage stamps, one at a time or fail to realize their housework might be done in a fraction of the time they spend now if there were some family cooperation and better planning.

Once the major time wasters have been identified, the next step is to break the pattern. Inertia has been locking us into this needless waste. Bodies in motion tend to remain in motion; any activity begun tends to continue. But if we break the pattern of this activity by stopping it, inertia begins to work for us; bodies at rest tend to remain at rest. And if we substitute one or more activities of our choice, these substituted activities tend to be continued and the benefits are cumulative. The activity or activities substituted are individual choices: reading, writing, taking a course, physical exercise, indoor games, visiting with friends or relatives, working with our hands, getting to know ourselves and our families better, painting, remodeling, arts, crafts, hobbies, developing an avocation, or whatever. We are not locked into any particular choice. And the sooner we begin, the sooner we benefit doubly, by substituting a positive in our lives for a negative. To begin is of vital importance. The energy flow derived from beginning an activity creates a momentum. It is this momentum, if unbroken, which can yield amazing results. For example, writing a book is much easier than is generally thought if the author works at it every day. Four hundred well-chosen words committed to paper each day will produce a nonfiction book in six months, a novel in nine. An interruption of the flow may postpone the process for weeks or months, possibly forever.

Once we have gained control over our own use of time, we are ready to deal with others who may disregard the value of our time. Limit the amount of time anybody may be permitted to usurp. We have seen one effective method of dealing with extended or inopportune telephone calls. Others must be made aware our time has a value. Be punctual and demand punctuality of others; never wait more than 30 minutes past the appointed time. Appointments with chronic latecomers must be made carefully and at a time and place convenient for us. Some people accommodate the lateness of others by setting such ap-

151

pointments fifteen minutes before they intend to arrive; I don't but I don't arrive early either.

Confirm appointments with anybody on whom you don't completely rely. This certainly includes hotels, airlines, car rental agencies, and the like. If written confirmation isn't feasible, at least find out with whom you are dealing. If busy professionals keep postponing appointments or won't set one at a near or convenient date, have somebody else set the appointment for you. It adds to your status and allows less flexibility for the professional's secretary if the dates you find convenient are not readily available. It also tends to reduce the time spent in the professional's waiting room. As relatively few people have others make their appointments, you have put yourself in a special category. And, of course, provide feedback: complain if the value of your time is ignored, and be equally appreciative of those who treat your time with proper respect. It is a mistake to be willing to absorb quietly these time losses whenever somebody chooses to inflict them.

Many people find it difficult to organize their day; they become enmeshed in relatively minor matters while what is important is left unattended. I believe it was a president of United States Steel who paid $25,000 for the solution to this problem: list what you want to accomplish each day in the order of its importance and simply begin at the top of the list and work down. Time is often equated with money; time isn't money, but if wasted, it will impoverish us as surely as if it were money we were thoughtlessly throwing away.

31 The Junking of Junk Mail

Over the years, most adults in this country have been repeatedly exhorted to get, do, join, enter, make, enjoy, save, earn, learn, send, repair, improve, be, buy, or sell in scores of unsolicited amazing, unique, breakthrough, revolutionary, unusual, fabulous, simple, daring, spectacular, unprecedented, step-by-step, free, guaranteed, and heavily punctuated opportunities on a wide variety of mail-order goods and services from amethysts to zinnias. Many of the offers are allegedly life-changing and almost all are at absurdly low prices, usually for a limited time only. The reason we receive our weekly pound of junk mail is that our name and address is bought and sold and rented and passed about from hand to hand, for profit, among a host of merchants throughout the country and as far away as the Orient.

This tonnage of mail (approximately two million tons annually) is certainly not free. Somebody has to pay for it and, not surprisingly, all of the costs are picked up by us: directly, in the price of the goods and services thus bought, and indirectly, in mail subsidies levied on us and wasted natural and human resources, even if we never respond to any direct-mail blandishments. These costs do not include the amounts lost on mail frauds and rip-offs.

Many pay in other ways that are most insidious and seductive. I know a man who was solicited to subscribe to a financial service. Included with the offer was a current sample of the company's wares, recommending the purchase of various securities for rapid, dramatic appreciation. This man happened to be among a substantial number of people who may haggle over the tax on a luncheon check but blithely commit large sums of money to stock market flyers if a strong enough appeal is made to greed. This single "free" piece of mail cost this individual more than seventy-five hundred dollars.

There is a strong argument to be made that this man had a right not to be influenced in this costly way, a right to be let alone. There was a time when a person's home was his castle and he was impervious to hazards and encroachments once inside his own premises. This is no longer true. We are bombarded every day by the rising clamor of commercialism right in our own homes. Commercial messages on television and radio, telephone pitchmen, door-to-door salespeople, neighbors (and their offspring) soliciting for a proliferation of charities, our portals are open to all and the din has become oppressive. This constant tapping at our brain pans is taking an increasing toll.

There are, of course, other abuses by some of the junk mailers. One common complaint is that merchandise paid for is never received. Another, that when the buyer attempts to exercise the money-back guarantee, the seller doesn't return the money. Another problem buyers face is that the seller may have none of the merchandise on hand at the time it is offered for sale. The seller is simply testing the market; if enough orders are received, the seller will then begin to set about producing the merchandise. This inevitably entails long delays between the time money is sent and merchandise is received, with the customers, in effect, financing the operation.

I am not minimizing the problems caused by these abuses or by any of the various mail frauds perpetrated by some of these companies. It is the repeated violation of our right of privacy, our right to the quiet enjoyment of our premises, I find most objectionable. It is these repetitive little incursions on our psyches, these attempts to interfere with and manipulate our thought processes, the cumulative pollution pouring into the societal bloodstream, the long-term effects of which are only now being seriously considered, that I find disturbing.

Privacy is a fragile treasure, all too easily taken from us without recourse. Oh, yes, there are some who may be quick to suggest that all junk mail may simply be thrown away unopened. Ignoring the sheer waste of resources and the other dollar costs, you would thereby eliminate the mental manipulations. Not true, for the direct-mail merchants, impatient to influence us, have learned to whisper their seductive messages to us on the envelopes! "Free gift inside," "Have More Money Than You Ever Thought

Possible!" "Live a Life of Indolence and Riches!!" "The Secret of a Longer, Healthier Life!!!" "Eternal Bliss Can Be Yours!" and so on. Who can long resist these attractive nuisances?

Fortunately, there are a few defensive techniques which can be mustered to deal with this relentless onslaught. If privacy is desired, door-to-door salespeople, soliciting neighbors and telephone pitchmen should be given no encouragement. Ever! Once you buy or contribute, your name has taken on a value as a prime prospect for more of the same and it is going to be added to an endless list of lists.

Unordered merchandise may be considered a gift in some states, but if you do return such items there is no point in paying the postage. Simply write "return to sender" on the mailing carton, obliterate your own name and address (this information is duplicated inside) and mail. Victims of mail fraud should contact the Postal Inspection Service (U.S. Post Office, Washington, D.C. 20260) or their local Post Office Inspection Service if paid for merchandise is not received or if money is not promptly returned after exercise of the money-back guarantee. Before involving the postal authorities, a registered letter to the merchant explaining the details of the transaction and your intention to notify the Postal Inspection Service if the matter is not attended to by return mail, can provide satisfaction. In a proper case, the Post Office can obtain the actual business address of a company which has given you only a post office box. Your letter can be especially effective if sent to this actual address and if you say that the Post Office has supplied the address and is waiting to hear whether or not you have been satisfied.

Some people, desperate to have their names removed

from mailing lists, have written "Deceased" on the mailing piece and sent it back to the Post Office. Others have attempted to staunch the flow of junk mail by returning it to the sender at the latter's expense in the hope this would encourage the company to remove their names from the lists. If this failed, weight was sometimes added or attached to the mailing piece (increasing the return postage) to emphasize its unacceptability. You can also have your name removed from mailing lists of companies that send sexually offensive material through the mail. On request, the Post Office will order your name removed from such a list. An effective way of eliminating about half of your junk mail quota is to ask the Direct Mail Advertisers Association at 230 Park Avenue, New York, N.Y. 10017, to inform their membership of your wish to have your name removed from all their lists.

The reduced volume of junk mail, if read, should be warily considered, particularly if payment for the order is demanded in advance. Ordering the merchandise on approval is, of course, less risky, although your name is almost undoubtedly going to appear on many mailing lists even if you decide to return the item.

Junk mail is easily identified, but if more positive identification is needed, simply use a first initial before your first name, such as "J" for junk if you ever order a mail order item. In this way, any mail later addressed to you with this first initial will clearly give itself away as junk mail and need not be opened. If "J" happens to be your first initial, it may be used as your middle initial. Those who find it difficult to throw away junk mail unopened may taper off by selecting the two most enticing envelopes of the week to open and throw the rest away. Later, this may be reduced to one, and then to zero.

Another approach is to open all junk mail without reading it. Collect all the return envelopes for later use in mailing payments of other companies' bills, crossing out the original address and attaching postage even if the envelope is postage paid to the original company. Any piece of junk-mail paper which has all or part of a side blank may be used as scrap paper. In this way, at least some of the wasted natural resources and solid waste may serve useful functions.

Many legitimate direct-mail advertisers do offer a wide assortment of products which may be highly valued by satisfied customers. On the other hand, millions of people have their psyches invaded at will by merchants and list brokers who buy, sell, and rent their names, repeatedly classifying and reclassifying each one in an effort to improve sales efficiency. Shouldn't these millions have a means of enforcing their right of privacy? Perhaps companies should be prohibited from selling and renting names. Why, for example, should a credit card company or a government bureau be permitted to sell our names and addresses, sometimes providing information about our age, income, and buying patterns? Perhaps an equitable balancing of our right to be let alone and the direct-mail advertiser's freedom to offer his wares could be found if we were given a convenient way of choosing to stop receiving any and all such mail on request. After all, the obscene telephone caller has a right of free speech, too, but society tries to limit the impact of that right on the psyches of his victims. An effort must be made to preserve those important quiet, contemplative moments too often shattered by this or that invasion of our prized privacy for profit.

32 How to Be Lucky

In a computerized, push-button society, the old fashioned virtue of perseverance, except in athletic competition, has fallen into disfavor. We crave immediate satisfaction, the easy and the quick; instant beverages, cameras, lotteries, junk and fast foods, conglomeratization, windfall profits, overnight success, massage parlors, gadgets, the rentable, the portable, prefabs.

Our span of attention is approaching that of a marigold seed. We try to "keep up" but there isn't enough time so we skim off less and less about more and more. We read headlines, digests, capsules, summaries, condensations, excerpts, annotations and we think in short sentences. We want things to happen "while we wait," demand "immediate pickup and delivery" and "same day" cleaning. We are impatient; we get bored. We want answers in 25 words or less and computer-printout summaries. We rely on gut feelings, vibes, the seat of the pants. We bluff a great deal because we don't have much knowledge and we are increasingly superficial, having forgotten yesterday before today is over. If we don't succeed at once, we fold the hand and try something else, elsewhere.

We are a nation of transient strangers, continually on the move. We live separated lives, isolated from our parents and our children. We change marriage partners, employment, and domiciles as if they were so many throwaway containers. With increasing frequency, our lifestyles are serial; we shed one identity and assume another with scarcely a backward glance and as easily as putting out the garbage.

We have more material possessions than any society in history but we are beginning to learn in a new and painful way that "more is less." Even our headlines now tell us that the man who has everything may have nothing to live for. Perhaps the significant reason for the phenomenal success of *Roots* is that it revealed our own rootlessness. Our national love affair with the automobile has also contributed to our footloose, "here today, gone tomorrow" instability. The closeness to the land characteristic of our pioneer forebears is notably absent today, environmentally filtered out of the national character. Character itself has become an anachronism, giving way to talent, real or apparent, and flair, a gossamer aptitude or rudimentary ability requiring little or no training and practically unmeasurable.

We use synthetics and accept "reasonable facsimiles." Appearance is often deemed more important than actuality and public relations has been elevated to both an art and a science. Purposeless, unmoored, our lives flapping like a loose sail, we seek escape in sex, drugs, and alcohol. We are desperate to believe in almost anything but ourselves and one another. We turn to highly paid gurus to introduce us to ourselves and face us in the right direction. And then we are off again and running. Like hungry squirrels, we are so busy darting here and there hoarding our acorns that we haven't the time to stop and enjoy the taste of food.

How do we put this flying circus behind us and find our way back into our own lives? If we pay close attention to ourselves and take sufficient time, we may be fortunate enough to discover a long-term, general purpose, something that can actually engage us, toward which we can begin to make our way. Once we have set our course, regardless of the difficulties, all we need do is keep moving in the right direction. Christopher Columbus, in his log, put it well: "This day, despite imminent threats of mutiny and storms, we sailed West because it was our course."

It may be argued that Columbus had a relatively easy task, and that if he continued to sail West, he couldn't miss. Without going into the hardships and the losses of that voyage, the point is neither can we miss if we keep sailing toward our goal. Thomas Edison provides another of a great many illustrative examples. A grammar-school dropout, Edison eventually held more than 1,300 United States and foreign patents, including patents covering dozens of basic inventions that transformed the world and which we take for granted every day. Yet Edison had an extraordinary failure rate. Thousands of his experiments ended in failure but he took careful note of what did not work and pushed on. Purpose and perseverance led him forward. In his quest for the incandescent light-bulb filament, the thousands of failures he amassed would have discouraged a battalion of people with less staying power. In accounting for his own success, Edison repeatedly turned aside all romantic suggestions that his accomplishments were the product of inspiration. He placed little faith in the instant genius who worked only when inspired or seized with flashing insight. "Genius," according to Edison, "is two per cent inspiration and ninety-eight per cent perspiration." He did not concern himself with what might be useful a century later. He confined his energies to the needs of the present.

The persistence and perseverance Edison exhibited in attaining his goals is the rule, not the exception, for success. Accomplishments achieved effortlessly, through luck or accident, rarely lead to further accomplishments. Success, without a method and hard work, is usually accompanied by self-doubt and guilt, barren ground for fulfillment and happiness.

While it may be conceded that perseverance toward an overall purpose is effective in overcoming all obstacles, few of us are aware of a grand design, a large purpose or pattern in our lives. If the many who are unaware were to substitute a series of project goals for a single generalized purpose and persevere toward each project goal, favorable results would be theirs. The project goal must be specific and involve a process and effort (doing something) over a period of time: "I want to write a particular book, play, etc.," not "I want to be a writer." Success will then be a by-product of the effort, not the goal. And the project goals may actually create a pattern that reveals our general purpose.

162

A great deal of discretion is recommended, so that few people become aware of your project goals. Telling people tends to dissipate energies better spent on the project. The opinion of others may dissuade you from following through or they may divert you. And inquiries about your progress are likely to lead to further energy loss, slippage, and blockage.

Our Anglo-Saxon system of jurisprudence, marvelous as it is, limits us to "our day in court." Other systems, of course, may not give us even that. But when this day, including all of our rights to appeal, is over, and we are turned away by the highest tribunal that will hear our case, we have had it. We have lost irrevocably; we will never win that case, even if the law is subsequently changed in our favor. Broad as our legal rights and protections are, they are strictly limited. In our daily lives, however, where we have an unlimited "right of appeal," we limit ourselves by dropping out if our initial efforts are not immediately availing. We are thus our own harshest judges.

If we were but to press on, to persevere toward our goals, we would not only be taking the most reliable route but we would be rewarded with a curious kind of bonus: good luck. This form of luck is not merely a function of chance; it can be created at will. It is most commonly produced when you multiply the possibilities for its presence by personal effort and concentrated attention in reaching a particular goal. However, this particular kind of luck does not penetrate doors or walls, and it invariably involves one or more other people. It is passed directly from somebody else to you if you are open and alert enough to receive it. It occurs unexpectedly but it is almost never visited upon the easily discouraged.

The relatively few people who know how to conjure up this kind of luck do so repeatedly and are sometimes envied and misunderstood by those who sit at home waiting in vain for good news to magically overtake their half-hearted efforts. But when all the results are in, the lucky ones, the people whose own efforts and good judgment brought themselves luck, are the biggest winners.

33 Homeless Away from Home

If an actor walks on stage and tells the audience he's starving and hasn't eaten in four days, we don't contradict him even if we saw him gorging himself on cannelloni at Sardi's after the last performance. We willingly suspend disbelief when we enter the theater (although we expect real towels, not props, in the washroom). Similarly, when we watch a magic show, we enjoy being taken in by illusion and misdirection. We know representations made by performers on stage are not always literally true, but unless the performance is so poor it negates itself, we are content to accept them until the final curtain has fallen and the house lights are up. Outside the theatre, it is wise to maintain a healthy skepticism toward oral representations. We are familiar with sales puffery and the extravagant claims of advertisers, and are wary of accepting these self-serving declarations at face value.

The written word, however, is much more commanding. How many millions of people, for example, continue to back away, puzzled but worried, from furniture tags on which is printed the unequivocal warning: "Do not remove this tag under penalty of law"? Although the message would seem to be addressed to sellers of these goods, no exceptions are mentioned so we anxiously obey, lest we be seen on the six o'clock news being led from our own homes in handcuffs.

Although I am as tractable as the next one about furniture tags, I have tilted, on occasion, with an even more unyielding obstacle: menus. Only after giving others the benefits of many doubts resulted in a long, almost unbroken skein of detriments to myself have I learned to question closely (while trying to appear cheerful and as casual as possible) even the most innocuous-looking staples I used to accept with confidence. For example, hotel dining rooms and restaurants all across the country offer some variation of "fresh squeezed" orange juice on their breakfast menus. Ungrammatical offerings should trigger more than usual alertness because sellers sometimes deliberately offer their wares ungrammatically so that if challenged they may attempt to take legal refuge behind the fact that ungrammatical usage has no precise meaning and therefore their statements are not provably incorrect.

Whether the juice is labeled "fresh squeezed" or "fresh, squeezed" or "freshly squeezed," when I sit down to breakfast in some at least pretty good hotel dining room or restaurant, I'm willing to go along and imagine sunshine, vitamin C, friendly orchard folk, good health, and a glorious day ahead that I'm going to toast shortly with a glass of some of that good juice. After all, a lot of money was spent to give me those images and it hasn't all been wasted. But more often than not the orange juice is frozen or has been poured from a can, the lid of which has had to be fished out by hand. And when the juice is actually squeezed on the premises, it has almost invariably been done no later than six in the morning. This guarantees that by breakfast time, virtually all of the vitamin C will have evaporated into the air in which it is soluble, eliminating the major tangible benefit. A small point? Perhaps, but if the plain meanings of words are allowed to be bent a full 180 degrees off course about an everyday breakfast item like orange juice, where will the line be drawn? Aren't deceptive menus exacting a daily kind of taxation without adequate representation and wasn't our country born in defiance of just such an attempt?

One could make a long list of deliberate and intentional menu misrepresentations: "Maine" lobsters that never spent a moment in the Pine Tree State, "Maryland" crabs that came from somewhere out the back door, "whipped cream" that is neither whipped nor cream, and scores of others. No doubt an irate citizenry, fed up with being misled in its most fundamental purchases, will eventually demand "truth in menu" laws to bring America's menu-makers into line.

Room service evokes an ease and elegance of a bygone era. But for those who enjoy a hearty breakfast, unless it is necessary to utilize the waiting time in the room or there is a strong preference for breakfast in bed, it is ordinarily ill-advised to hazard the vagaries of room service. Errors and omissions are not easily corrected and by the time they are, the rest of the meal is cold or out of synch or it is too late to

167

enjoy it. However, if room service, with its higher costs and risks, is attempted, it is an obvious advantage to place the order with somebody who prefers, however slightly, that you enjoy the meal. (Hindsight is useful here, of course.) This commendable service orientation improves the chances the order will be correctly transmitted to the cook but by no means assures your receiving the breakfast you chose.

A relatively simple item like two boiled, unshelled three-minute eggs, slowly and carefully ordered two or three slightly different ways to improve comprehension, and correctly repeated by the order taker, has produced shelled and unshelled eggs from almost raw to hard-boiled and a variety of other egg dishes, barely missing eggs Florentine. Leaving the eggs in their shells keeps them cleanest and allows them to "cook" a bit longer, which is the way I prefer them. As often as not, my preference is ignored. There are, in fact, at least a couple of large hotel chains that do not offer and will not serve guests ordering room service boiled eggs of any kind unless a strong appeal is made to the manager.

Another small point? Probably, but attention to details is what makes a few hotels great and others poor. I don't know of a single hotel in the world that has the proper respect for the individual differences of their guests. For example, I have never been asked for my preferred rising time. If that were made a routine part of reservations and registration, it would create an opportunity to segregate the earlier risers on the highest floors, grading guest rising preferences down to the lowest floors for the latest risers. As earlier risers tend to retire earlier, they would be less likely to be prevented from falling asleep by more frequent pre-midnight hotel and street traffic noises on a higher floor. Those on the top floor would have the added advantage of having nobody above them, eliminating overhead noise. Early risers would also be spared the disturbances of late retirers and, in turn, would spare later risers from room and plumbing noises and the slamming of doors on leaving in the morning. Nor would the cleaning and housekeeping staffs be disturbing the sleep of the guests if they simply worked downward from the highest floors, adjusting their schedules to the guests' instead of forcing an arbitrary schedule on their guests. If enough people started asking for this and similar minor shows of concern, maybe the hotel management would get the message.

I have also found that "do not disturb" signs hung on hotel doors are about as effective against passkeys as dental floss against rabies. If such signs were designed to indicate a time after which they would be inoperative (like the clock face hung on shop doors which tells customers when the shop will reopen) and this were respected by hotel staff and guests alike, about 90 percent of the intrusions could be eliminated without loss. In the absence of some civilizing improvements it is curious that experienced travel-writers find so many hotels and restaurants "delightful" and "charming." It would be of much greater service to the public if these professionals or some other perceptive travelers brought a list of shortcomings to the attention of top management and reserved their praise for the truly deserving.

At the close of a particularly pleasant and/or productive day away from home, have you ever looked forward to a good dinner, perhaps in the best-appointed hotel dining room; or maybe you preferred to order the meal from room service and step into a hot tub or shower, allowing enough time so you were comfortably in your robe when the meal arrived? My first choice of entrees under such circumstances is usually medium rare roast prime ribs of beef with the bone attached, which I've ordered many times—specifying that unless the beef is prime (as described on the menu) and the bone is actually attached, I'd be happy to order something else, (which seems fair enough to me)—only to be served, about half the time, nonprime beef with or without a bone attached, from rare to extremely well done. Sometimes a bone that had never been attached to the beef intended for me has been placed adjacent to it.

Until the traveling and dining public becomes aware of, and begins to assert, its rights, second-rate treatment at first-class prices will remain the standard. "Truth in menu" and other "truth" legislation will help and a concerted effort should be made at the local level to demand the whole truth in lieu of the whole cloth. In the meantime, we are much on our own.

In reserving a hotel room and again upon checking in, I tell the person addressed I'd like a quiet room, away from the elevator and other traffic. Room-service meals are ordered with as many specifics as will make my preferences clear. It is by being specific that wrong impressions, deliberately or innocently engendered, can be corrected. Words are only words, not the goods and services for which we are paying. Outside the theatre, words should be "wrung out" so that the latent ambiguities are eliminated. It is always a mistake to confuse the moon with the finger pointing at the moon. I usually ask for an estimated time for delivery of meals, laundry, and the like and the name of the person to whom I am speaking on the telephone. Both of these precautions tend to improve performance. If you wish to have a bed-board or any other housekeeping item, it should be requested as early as possible (with names and delivery times). Complaints about faulty air conditioners, plumbing, television sets or other objections to the room should be made at once, and another room sought if the defect(s) cannot be cured quickly. Good service should be appreciated and, in addition to payment, those who are particularly able or caring should be mentioned to management. It is important that strong approval and disapproval be given expression.

All requests should be made in a courteous, firm, clear, and expectant manner as if there is no doubt in your own mind as to the propriety of the request.

Getting what we pay for away from home isn't always easy. If we are alert and ask for our reasonable entitlement and shun and complain when it isn't forthcoming and praise and recommend when it is, in time the mountain will begin to move. A great deal of progress, for example, has been made by organized action with respect to restricting smoking on common carriers, in elevators, and in stores selling food. Much more remains to be done.

34 Increasing Your Delegations

The delegation to others of tasks within their competence is a basic and most useful management technique. By freeing himself or herself from needlessly spending large accumulations of time on a variety of matters that don't require his or her personal execution, the productive executive is able to concentrate effectively on the true management functions of his or her job. This valuable procedure, well recognized in business, is largely ignored outside of the office or plant, where it is no less useful.

A little thought can provide us with variations, refinements, and extensions of this technique to help us exchange the oceans of time and energy we needlessly waste in our daily lives, bogged down in a welter of easily delegated details, for opportunities to enjoy some refreshing leisure or to pursue any other goals we choose. It should be made clear that in delegating such details we do not intend to attempt to fob off on anybody a single task which is properly ours. This would include Tom Sawyer's painting of the fence, for, although it may be drawing too fine a moral line, that job was specifically assigned to Tom by Aunt Polly as a punishment.

One application of this delegating technique involves those frequently encountered situations in which we are faced with unattractive alternatives. We usually choose "the lesser of the two evils." Delegating, however, gives us the opportunity to create a third possibility not immediately apparent. Let us suppose, for example, we've gone to an expensive restaurant for dinner with some friends or business associates and the check is presented. The check is rather large, with more than enough margin for error, and we are aware mistakes sometimes occur in these situations. We would like some assurance we are being billed the correct sum but we would also like to avoid the cumbersome and somewhat embarrassing task of crosschecking the bill and the menu. We certainly don't intend to interrupt the flow of the after-dinner conversation at the table to ask who ordered what (so the check may be erroneous despite correct addition) and, in fact, we'd much prefer to socialize with our friends or business associates. We seem to be faced with a choice of paying a possibly incorrect bill or eliminating ourselves from a conversation in which we wish to participate in order to do a somewhat embarrassing and inconclusive chore.

We may finesse this dilemma by delegating the responsi-

173

bility for the correctness of the dinner check. The person to ask would typically be somebody who benefits from the transaction. In this example, we might call the captain or the waiter to the table (either of whom is actually in a better position than we to verify the check without disturbing any of the diners) and politely ask whether he'd mind having somebody doublecheck the bill. Having thus chosen neither of the "two evils," we are free to resume the conversation. The "somebody" will probably be the captain or the waiter but regardless of who actually does the rechecking, the second time around there is an excellent chance it will be done without any mistakes. Whether or not there are corrections (which more often than not, if my experience is typical, will reduce the check), a polite thank you will suffice.

An awareness of this technique can help defend us from the excessive, improper, and unnecessary delegations of others. For example, suppose we get calls from friends or associates who request a favor of us that requires the cooperation of a third party. We are being delegated to do something on behalf of the caller. We may have to relay messages back and forth between the caller and the third party, inconveniencing the latter and ourselves and building a debt of gratitude or obligation which will have to be repaid later.

This kind of situation, viewed as an attempt to delegate us, practically resolves itself. If we choose to be of help, and the caller and the third party are acquainted, we may "undelegate" ourselves by suggesting the caller speak directly with the third party. The same approach is appropriate if the third party is an easily consulted reference source. If, however, the third party is not readily accessible to the caller, we may limit our involvement, as well as the total number of calls involved, by telling the caller we will ask the third party whether he or she would be willing to speak with the caller directly.

Other effective means of delegating include pooling, sharing, bartering, and hiring. Any combining of goods and/or services toward a common purpose may be considered a pooling arrangement. A familiar example of pooling is the car pool, in which several people bound for the same general destination ride together, with resultant savings for all. Vehicles and drivers are usually alternated on some agreed-upon basis, although sometimes a driver may be paid instead. Suburban parents often alternate picking up and delivering their young children and those of their neighbors on their respective ways to and f·om school. Some people alternate dinners at each other's houses or pool their contributions in preparing a church supper.

Sharing involves joint or alternate use of goods and/or services. Two or more individuals or families might decide to share a vacation home, for example, at the same time or at alternate times. By combining in this way, each of the parties may enjoy all the use of the property he wishes with a savings in operating expenses or rent and a division of certain necessary chores.

Bartering involves the exchange of some goods and/or services for other goods and/or services either at the same time or for future delivery. An auto mechanic might exchange his services in repairing an accountant's car for the latter's services in preparing the former's tax returns; or two owners of houses in different parts of the world might exchange the use of their respective houses on some agreed-upon basis.

Pooling, sharing, and bartering involve situations in which those who delegate typically also act as delegates of others, either at the same time or at a future time, to the mutual benefit of all the parties.

Finally, there are scores of ways to delegate by hiring, as illustrated in any metropolitan classified telephone directory. Thousands of service people (and others) are available to perform a wide variety of delegated tasks from ordinary household chores to some of the most exotic callings.

The important point is that we don't have to be under pressure to do everything ourselves. We tend to overrate the value of our own personal contribution, expecting snarls, mishaps, and disasters if we are not on hand to get things to run smoothly. But when we are out of town on business or pleasure, or otherwise unavailable, all, mercifully, miraculously, is not lost. By selectively delegating many of the unnecessary responsibilities we have allowed to pile up and clutter our lives, we can eliminate a great deal of stress and create a desirable flexibility in our lives.

35 Sociomycin

Doctors often prescribe a broad-spectrum antibiotic to combat a nonspecific bacterial infection. So, too, in the absence of a specific remedy, we may use a broad-spectrum approach to protecting ourselves from a number of societal incursions: sociomycin. In the course of everyday social and commercial dealings, attempts to regulate our conduct are made through laws, rules, principles, policies, procedures, facts, definitions, precedents, and personalities. Often this catalog of societal "controllers" works in our favor, whether or not we are fully aware of precisely how it operates. Sometimes, however, some of these factors may be brought to bear in a manner detrimental to our interests. We may absorb each loss or inconvenience or we may attempt to defend ourselves and contest this or that imposition of the penalty with which we are faced.

But defend and contest how? These transactions occur at the speed of life. Like disease germs that are everpresent but become clinically harmful only when our resistance is otherwise lowered, inadequate and unfair treatment is commonplace and our turn is almost inevitable in the hurly burly of rubbing up against rudeness, indifference, and incompetence and its equally unattractive mutations and permutations. I have proposed a number of solutions to specific common problems in this vein but it would be delusive to attempt an immediate practical solution for every conceivable wrong an army of malefactors might commit. In addition to whatever specific remedies we can carry with us, we need something more, a theoretical approach, which can be used at our discretion against a broad spectrum of common offenses. Eliminating legal controversies from our consideration, which are properly beyond the scope of this book, with what curatives can we stock our little black bag to help us face a less than perfect world?

We can avoid a host of unpleasant consequences and improve our position by introducing some new element into the transaction to distinguish our particular situation from the class of cases which it superficially appeared to resemble, and to which the burden we wish to avoid might properly attach. Lawyers have thus attempted to "distinguish" cases for decades. Sometimes, of course, they introduce a specious distinction, a so-called distinction without a difference.

For example, I once owned a majority interest in a small

corporation into which, I discovered belatedly, stock in another company which my corporation accepted as readily saleable and which it valued at approximately the bid price, was "frozen." That is, I discovered the stock was not readily convertible into cash at or near its market price. When I pointed out that my corporation would not have paid so much for the stock if it hadn't been misinformed that the stock was saleable, and demanded a discount for the stock in its impaired condition, I was told by a lawyer who attempted to justify the original valuation of the stock that when my corporation had accepted the stock as saleable it *was* saleable, although not "sellable." Needless to say, this alleged distinction was unacceptable, but the technique itself was faultless.

I heard a youngster asked to do a household chore by a parent reply: "It's not my turn to do that." An excellent distinction, which combines a definite, specific, and strong implication of refusal without directly challenging parental authority; an appeal to fair play and a sense of justice (like the formulation suggested earlier: "In all fairness!"); and a suggestion of where to look for a substitute to do the chore. Plus economy: seven one-syllable words!

A common mistake is to attempt to frame a reply before the basis on which the negative effect is being imposed is fully understood. Is it a law, rule, principle, policy, procedure, fact, definition, precedent, or personality that binds you? Is it verbal or written and on what authority is it based? Once you understand the text and the context, determine whether you can distinguish yourself out of its nettles. If not, you face the harder task of challenging the text and/or its purported authority over you.

Proceed slowly and wait for responses from the other side if you are dealing face to face or on the telephone.

Learn to interpret the responses so you understand what is being implied as well as expressed. In conversational encounters, do not use up all of your argumentative ammunition in the initial salvo. This avoids placing the other person in the position of having to overrule himself immediately, which may be expecting too much. Try to find areas of agreement early. If you can think of nothing better with which to space your side of the conversation, you may simply repeat variations of: "We must think of some way to (state your objective here)."

If others present are also affected try to remove yourself and the person whose help you seek from their immediate presence. You don't want to make your task harder by having to convince all the others that your needs are more urgent than theirs, as well as the person who can help you. For example, if you are at an airport and your flight has been canceled, many other passengers are also affected. This is a "fact" situation, not a "policy" unfairly applied to you. You will want to act quickly to obtain a preference before there is none left. Enlist the help of the agent on duty to direct you to the person best able to help you get to your destination (if that is your objective). Don't make demands; you are asking for help. That can be made clear by simply saying: "I need your help." State your objective and its urgency, distinguishing yourself from others who appear to be similarly situated. Don't state your interpretation of the solution if you trust their expertise.

If you are stranded by a canceled flight, tell somebody who can help you where you want to go and when you have to arrive; don't mastermind which flights you will need. Knowledgeable airline employees are in a better position to figure your routing than you are. Once you have stated your urgent need to get to your destination by a certain deadline and they are aware of why you have been prevented, you can determine whether the person addressed and ostensibly helping you is "service oriented" or indifferent and/or incapable of helping you. If the person can help and wants to, keep checking with that person. If not, thank the person for his time and ask for somebody else. If the person wants to help but can't, he will be able to direct you to the person best able to help you, who, you may suggest, may or may not be present at the airport.

I've had magical results with allegedly impossible problems in one call to the main office in town. In a similar situation, I reserved a car from an auto rental company. When I arrived to pick up the car, there was no record of my reservation and "no cars available." I attempted to distinguish my case factually but soon realized I was not dealing with a service-oriented person, a common failing among service personnel. I called a company executive long distance, explained the problem and my need, and soon had the use of a Cadillac at the price of a Ford. A good approach doesn't guarantee a solution every time but it improves the odds and with success comes a certain confidence and flair in handling these kinds of situations.

A suggestion has been made in cases like the airline and auto rental examples, where many people face a similar problem and only a limited number of them can be helped, that a so-called Dutch auction be held to determine who is helped. In a Dutch auction, the article being auctioned is put up at a higher price than anyone will pay and the price is gradually reduced until an acceptable value is found. If several airplane seats or rental cars, for example, are available, but not enough to satisfy all those upset by the shortage, the first to bid the descending price goes on his way and the auction continues at descending prices.

Unfortunately, in the Dutch auction, money is the sole criterion and its relative value may not truly determine need.

You may occasionally be told (or it may be implied) others are also in disadvantaged positions and the company plans to treat all of these people equally at a later time and you, therefore, cannot get an immediate preference. "If we did this for you, then we'd have to do it for everyone," the company spokesman might say. That person should be told you appreciate the company's sense of fair play under the pressure of the particular situation. However, it should be explained that you did everything you could to guarantee the availability of the car, airline seat, or whatever, that many of the others left to chance. And the reason you took such care was the importance of whatever it is to you. Some of the others may not even have much desire to take this trip and are doing it under some pressure; others are on company time and would be happy for the opportunity to do something else. For you, it's top priority and to be really fair, you deserve all the help this person and the company can provide.

Simply asking for clarification and help distinguishes your case from that of all those who accept losses and foul-ups without question or complaint. Persistence also distinguishes your case from those of people who give up easily and accept a poor result after a perfunctory, half-hearted attempt to improve it. A woman in Pennsylvania, who'd bought a Japanese car that turned out to be defective, tried in every way she could think of to remedy the situation, with no result—until one of her many carbon copies of complaint letters, addressed to former Prime Minister Tanaka, struck a responsive chord. The Prime Minister arranged for a new engine to be installed by her local dealer. A woman in Florida wrote to me about a defective organ she'd purchased, and described how all of her efforts to have it replaced had fallen on deaf ears. I suggested she write to the manufacturer's management, sending carbon copies to the manager of the store where she had bought the organ, various governmental and private agencies, the local "Action" reporter, several consumer-oriented organizations, the advertising department of the periodical in which she saw the advertisement for the organ, the state attorney general, and her representatives in Congress. I suggested she include a summary of the facts, her efforts, and the company's responses to that point. The woman pressed on and got a new organ. If good results are obtainable on big-ticket items like these, they can certainly be achieved with items of lesser value.

In how many additional particulars can you distinguish your case? Do you have a natural preference by virtue of a favorable and/or longstanding business and/or personal relationship with the company or its management? Was it the intent of the rule to include your situation or was your case not even contemplated by the rulemakers? Are you specifically or implicitly excepted, or excluded from the force of the rule? Has the rule expired? Would the application of the rule to your situation create bad publicity, actionable damages, or other jeopardy for the business, the rulemaker, or the rule enforcer? Can you get a temporary postponement from the adverse effect with which you are confronted? For example, if you arrive at a hotel late at night with a reservation for six nights and are told there are no rooms available, can you get a room for one night only? Often, if you make it clear you will move into any available room the next day, and that if no room can be found for you the following day, you will leave, you will be put up for the night. After a night's sleep and a good breakfast, you are in a better position to deal with the situation than after a long, tiring trip. You will also be dealing with other people, the day shift, and they or top management (also more readily available during daylight hours) may be able to help you. If you cannot distinguish yourself out of the rule, can you attack the rule itself? Is it legally permissible to impose it on you; is its application against public policy or uncompetitive? Is it unconstitutional, is it antiquated, is it superseded by events, or is it being applied in an arbitrary or discriminatory manner?

The incidence of social and commercial wrongs inflicted on a growing populace steadily mounts. The graceless insult, the gratuitous shove, the silence of numberless limbos and holding patterns into which urgent matters are swept by uncomprehending specialists, to languish unattended and be forgotten—these daily offenses are threatening to reach a critical mass beyond which their dehumanizing effects might well become irreversible. Not a panacea, sociomycin can nevertheless provide an ameliorating salve for a number of wounds which would otherwise remain untreated.

36 The Upper Hander's Starter Kit

Browsing through toy stores before Christmas, I was struck with the variety and range of complexity of hobby kits for sale. Travel was a big feature. Space capsules, motor cars, locomotives and cabooses, diving bells, sailing ships, submarines, and aircraft were all well represented. Communication was also popular. Radios were in abundance, from crystal to wrist. Telephones, too, and even the intricacies of television were not too difficult to be packaged in parts and pieces and spelled out in simple directions to be wrestled with by the hour.

There were kits aplenty; whole warehouses of them, from derricks and hoists to computers. Their future owners might well be able to put them together and get them to function. And their youthful fantasies and imaginations might even be nourished with visions of space explorations and mechanics, and electricity. All well and good. But which kit among the lot would protect them from even a single sneering sommelier? What kit could be purchased that offered the slightest hint about muzzling an abusive clerk or locating an elusive executive and cutting an immediate voice path through space to his inner, suddenly attentive ear, or hip-tossing a deceptive merchant or semiretired bureaucrat? And what of their elders? If some beneficent kit manufacturer were to develop and market such a line of kits to prepare young minds for the real and terrifying world, would adults be denied their benefits solely on the discriminatory basis of age?

As a spur to progress, I began to envision a whole series of such kits, ranging from a rudimentary (and least expensive) model, through the deluxe to the highly specialized and custom-built. A practical model would have to be much more "affordable" than a Cordoba and lighter than a full field pack. It would contain an effective mix of preventives, antidotes, and sockdolagers for a wide band of otherwise troublesome encounters. Willy Loman might leave home base armed with only a smile and a shoe shine but he lived in far less turbulent times. We would need something more sophisticated, of stouter construction, harder-edged.

A component of imaginative status symbols would, of course, be included in all of our models. People have been impressing one another for centuries with entire catalogs of artifacts, but sheer size and scale, bigness, grandiosity alone is usually enough to inspire awe and respect among the impressionable. For example, I was once arranging to film a legendary Hollywood producer at work. He couldn't have been more cooperative until I suggested we shoot some footage in his office, at which point he balked. His own desk, it developed, wasn't big enough to impress the millions of people who would see him behind it. It wasn't until I offered studio facilities and assured him I would rent a suitable desk that he agreed to make himself available. As long as the money was to be spent, I told him he might select any style of desk he wished. It made no difference, he replied, as long as it was the biggest desk I could find. It cost $700 to rent the desk I picked out for a few hours, but this man, who had given us scores of great films and had won about every award in the business in a career that spanned decades, would not be seen by the public without the symbolic prop of a huge desk.

The "movie capital of the world" has paid big dues for bigness: big houses with big stables and big swimming pools and big garages for big cars and big staffs and big yachts and big mortgages. Its studios have been turning out words, pictures, and songs for 50 years that have conditioned us, with their sprocket-holed messages, to believe we can be anything we want to be. The convincers, it appears, are the most convinced. For a price, almost anything, wives, children, and close friends included, can be rented, like props, and disposed of almost as easily.

We, too, can create certain impressions with the status symbols in our kit. Our symbols will be evocative and representational, and substitute legerdemain and penumbra for size and cost. We will employ not vast estates and big cars to create our effects but personal symbols that can be worn or carried or affixed. Initialed scarves and collector's plates and other mass-produced merchandise may have cachet with some, but our status symbols will denote achievement, not purchase, and represent attainments bestowed on only a favored few.

Before we proceed, a word of caution. We are now entering the twilight zone where illusion and fraud will overlap with the slightest misstep. A bold-faced announcement in large type to this effect would be included in all models of our kits and be prominent on the boxes themselves. Buyers would be cautioned not to enter this sensitive area without consulting their own legal and spiritual advisors for specific advice and counsel. In any event, our props would not be actual Distinguished Flying Crosses or Legion of Honor decorations or other such badges of honor easily obtainable at pawn shops and surplus stores. That would be both fish (in a barrel) and foul. We would do better to create our own nonspecific lapel decorations out of bits of colored ribbons or metal castings. And we would never make false claims under any circumstances! But as a barbershop tan may create the illusion of time spent in the sun (and, according to one of the world's wealthiest men, add 5 percent to your side of a deal), or makeup may make up natural deficits, so our props create this or that impression.

For example, on a commercial flight, a flight bag carried abroad that has "obviously" been through customs in Angola, Vietnam, Israel, Egypt, and Burundi or Zaire, and a few foreign dispatches, some blank cables which could be written en route on your portable typewriter, and perhaps some telex paper, would establish you as a war correspondent or newsperson. Dress would be optional, but serviceable, rugged, and casual might add a certain touch on a long flight.

Similarly, a couple of scripts in an envelope, out of

which a stop watch and/or a lens on a lanyard is permitted to poke carelessly, would establish you as a director; or a small pouch of "precious" stones and a jeweler's loupe would identify you as a gem dealer.

And if it is relatively simple to set the stage in these everyday theaters of encounter as to who you are, it is even easier to establish where you are. All the sound effects used to advantage in the old radio dramas are available on records and can be rerecorded (or recorded live if you prefer) on a cassette for convenience and portability. If, for example, you are late to a dinner party or getting home, your lame excuse about a car breakdown can be made sprightly if the background sounds of a highway or garage accompany your telephoned explanation.

You might as easily provide the sound effects of a brokerage office, the country club pool, a barber shop, a rehearsal of a play, a hospital, bus and airline terminals, railroad stations, piers, a crackling fire at the lodge, an office, a party, an office party, a restaurant, a tennis match, a ranch, a hotel lobby, a police station, or almost any location which has a distinctive, easily recognized sound, with the possible exception of a Trappist monastery. A character in a motion picture released a few years ago used the recorded sound of a vicious dog in another room to create for visitors the illusion she was protected by a guard dog on the premises. If the woman had said, in the direction of the taped cassette in the next room, "Down, Grendl!" after the person at the door heard the initial barking, and the sound were to subside into growling followed by silence or the sounds of a jingling dog license and paws padding across a room, the image would have been strengthened.

For bargaining power with noisy neighbors, how about the sound of a pneumatic drill or the crash and clatter of garbage cans recorded on an audio cassette? Placed as close as possible to the wall or ceiling of the offending neighbor, and played a few times at high volume for about a half hour while you are out, even the most stubborn and indifferent individuals often become conciliatory. At first, of course, your neighbor may wonder how such sounds got so close to home but he will soon begin to respond and become noticeably more tractable after the initial surprise. Until this sort of innovation, apartment dwellers had been completely at the mercy of their upstairs neighbors. These effects, designed and intended to be used only for purposes of retaliation and negotiation, provide a needed equalizer. If the neighbor has a dog, the recorded sounds of a dog whistle, played at high volume, will soon have the dog barking loudly enough to awaken your inconsiderate neighbors whenever you wish. Again, this measure is to be used only as an overture to a composing of differences.

The possibilities for inclusion in the Upper Hander's Starter Kit are myriad. Stick-ons can be attached to automobile windows, the more impressive looking and unfamiliar the better, or foreign license plates and other status tags may add a touch of distinction. As earlier suggested, an instant camera has a great deal of utility, *mano a mano,* in photographing wrongdoers and animating them into better grace.

The Upper Hander's Starter Kit is clearly an idea whose time will long be with us. We may expect these items to become available not only at survival shops everywhere and to be featured in mail-order catalogs, but to become the basis of required laboratory courses in secondary schools, colleges, and universities, and an important catalyst in fostering healing, reconciliation, and brotherhood throughout our troubled world.

190

37   Lemon Sweetener

It is the unusual new car that is free of defects. Often, as we know from the millions of cars that are recalled, owners are unaware of many of these defects, which can be dangerous, even deadly. But even when a new automobile owner is painfully aware of serious mechanical failure it is difficult to get prompt, effective relief. Some owners, in despair, have buried their automobiles in elaborate ceremonies. Others have driven them about, advertising them as "lemons"; some have parked these three-dimensional advertisements near dealers' showrooms in an effort to convince sellers to reconsider their anguished cries for help. Here's an approach a friend of mine used: I gave him some encouragement and suggested asking for more than was minimally acceptable and sending out an impressive sheaf of carbon copies, but he took up the cudgels himself. He chose this approach.

April 28, 1975
REGISTERED MAIL
Mr. A_____
(blank) Distributors

_____

_____, California

Dear Mr. A. _____:

On Monday, April 21, 1975, Mr. B_____ met with me and my attorney at _____ to evaluate the present condition of the new car which I had purchased from your showroom for my wife in September, 1974. I understood that Mr. B_____ is one of the finest technical experts in Los Angeles and he is an employee of the _____ Motor Company. Mr. B_____ confirmed to me, to my lawyer, to the General Sales Manager at your company, and to my salesman that the car was still leaking transmission oil. I had asked Mr. B_____ to confirm that fact—that the car still leaked transmission oil—to you.

At this point I would like to review with you the history of problems we have had with this car since its purchase in September, 1974, up to and including the April 21st meeting with Mr. B_____ where he confirmed that the car is continuing to leak transmission oil.

The history is as follows:

192

The (_____) car that we purchased from you in September, 1974 was new. From the beginning we noticed that the car was smoking; smoke came out of the area surrounding the headlights and the space between the hood and the fenders. When we reported the appearance of the smoke, we were told that we were warming up the car improperly. My wife received instructions on the use of the choke and was told that if we followed these instructions the car would no longer smoke. The instructions were followed to the letter and still the car continued to smoke. We brought the car to your chief mechanic, who said that a transmission hose near the top part of the engine was improperly routed next to a hot pipe and that simply replacing that hose and rerouting it would eliminate the smoking. We were told that this hose was not available from you and would have to be gotten through another source and rerouted. We left the car with the chief mechanic again and the "repair was made." My wife took the car out and the car continued to smoke. After each repair, we were told the car had been road tested. . . .

[He included a detailed history here.]

As you can now see, there is a serious question of my wife's safety involved and I will under no circumstances allow her safety to be in question. The car has proved unrepairable. It is not the brand-new car, free of trouble, I paid for. As you know, I have filed a consumer complaint with the Los Angeles Bureau of Consumer Affairs, asking them to investigate this matter.

I am prepared to pursue this matter until, as a customer of (_____) Distributors, I receive satisfaction. Because

193

my wife's safety is now involved, and because of her fear of driving this particular car with its history of service repairs, its explosions and fire, its smoking, and after eight "repairs" for the same problem, I am now again asking that the car be replaced or my money refunded. On April 21st, the General Sales Manager, after hearing Mr. B_____'s confirmation that the car still leaked transmission oil, again refused to replace the car. He wanted to repair it again!

As you know, I am a single customer and (_____) is a major international corporation, but I want you to know I will do whatever is necessary to ensure and guarantee my wife's safety. She is frightened of driving this car! It has proved unrepairable and I will go to any lengths to ensure her safety—*in advance, and before a tragedy occurs.*

I will not release this letter to the press and other media this time. I will however, wait two weeks from the date of this letter for you and the (_____) Corporation to make a decision as to how you will remedy this situation.

Again, I ask you, in fairness, to replace this car or refund my money.

Respectfully and most sincerely,

_____

cc: Mr. _____ _____,
       Chairman _____ _____

       _____

Mr. _____ _____,
   President _____ _____
   _____

Mr. _____ _____,
   _____ _____ _____

Mr. Tom Rosch, Director, Bureau of Consumer Affairs, Federal Trade Commission, Washington, D.C.

Mr. Dale Sekovich, Federal Trade Commission; Los Angeles, California

Mr. Evelle Younger, Attorney General, State of California

Bureau of Consumer Affairs, Los Angeles; Case number _____

Mr. Thomas Rees, U.S. Congressman

Mr. John Tunney, U.S. Senator, California

Mr. Alan Cranston, U.S. Senator, California

Bureau of Automotive Repairs, Consumer Complaint Division; Sacramento, California

Better Business Bureau, Los Angeles, California

My friend and his wife did not get a new car but they received prompt action at last. A new transmission was installed and the seat belts were finally replaced. The car seemed to be running smoothly, at last report.

38 Duet or Duel?

Life may be looked at as a continuing duet in which the individual and his or her environment each plays one of the two parts. This interaction may be harmonious but sometimes one of the parts upsets the balance by becoming dominant and the harmony is destroyed.

If, for example, you are too passive in playing your part, the environment will begin to take control and wear you down. You will be subjected to a number of harsh effects. Your world will impinge on you in unexpected and unpleasant ways which may seem to be coincidental or accidental. Such reverses are not a matter of chance, bad fortune, or destiny. Even as lowering your resistance to disease, by malnourishment or prolonged stress, for example, leaves you vulnerable to ever-present disease germs that would otherwise be innocuous, a too passive approach to living leaves you open to an invasion from without that would normally be quite harmless.

On the other hand, a relatively small percentage of people take an overly active and self-assertive approach to life. They continually strive for positions of power. They seek to control and dominate events and other people. Their efforts are directed at bending and molding the environment to their will. Although these people are generally regarded as successful and are sometimes leaders in their respective fields, they are usually unloved and unfulfilled. When these insatiable power drives are present in an individual who also lacks a sense of humor about himself, his company is particularly oppressive and abrasive and he is often shunned, even by his own colleagues and family.

Happily, the past need not determine the future for any of us. Life is a process, not a product, and it is therefore open to continuous change. It is unlike a game in which each of the players begins with equal forces and rigid rules determine all of the action. It is also unlike a can of edited film that always plays itself out the same way, no matter how much the audience may wish it otherwise. Our own lives are not fully scripted, much less edited. By putting ourselves into the equations of our respective lives, we have an opportunity to determine the results. With surprisingly few exceptions, there are no givens in life and any that are self-imposed or imposed from without may be challenged and changed. Life is not a final examination for which we may find the answers in the back of the book. The answers are to be found in life, in living, in making choices, in taking chances. There are no meanings apart from life.

When I was a child (and for too long thereafter) a great many situations seemed to be laden with immutable givens and I had no idea I could challenge them. My first thought was to conform myself to them, to follow them, to work within their arbitrary limitations. The result was a series of unrewarding transactions and small personal disasters that narrowed and clotted my life unnecessarily. If somebody, for example, had instructed me to take a message to Garcia and to do it quickly, I would have been off and running in all directions. I never would have thought to ask where Garcia was or how I was to get there or how I would recognize him or why he couldn't simply be telephoned.

When I became interested in consumer complaints, I began to learn that the givens are only the starting points, never the final destinations. Recently my wife and I spent a weekend at a resort hotel with some friends. We overslept the breakfast hours on Sunday. I was told room service was only serving continental breakfast (a roll and coffee) and we would have to wait at least an hour. I asked for the person in charge of room service and explained in a pleasant tone that the only reason we'd missed breakfast in the dining room with our friends was that we'd been kept awake into the wee hours by inconsiderate and noisy guests (which disturbances we were finally able to have quelled). The result was that he personally delivered two marvelous breakfasts to my wife and me in less than 20 minutes.

By putting yourself into the equation of any situation you can affect or change the equation. I have seen people shivering in restaurants when the air conditioning had been turned up too high and its effects were increasingly felt as the crowd thinned out. All they had to do was ask for the air conditioning to be turned down to a comfortable level.

The world is not taking notes on your every move, your every thought, preparatory to striking a good conduct medal when you have suffered enough. You are responsible for yourself. It is a mistake to put your life in the charge of others and not take your own turn at bat. Too often people remove themselves from the lineup. They voluntarily give up their chance to swing at the ball, to savor the experience, usually because they fear they may fail at whatever it is. And one voluntary removal creates an impetus for others until such people become habituated to withdrawing more and more from life itself.

If these people would stop and take note of their own feelings they would know they are not making themselves happy by this approach. If the melody inside you is not to your liking you can call for another tune. It's up to you. It's your move. You can modify your own behavior and even your environment to bring it and yourself into a better balance, a happier mode. It's a little like a seesaw. If you're too light and the other side (the environment) is too heavy, don't just sit up there in the air, high and dry. Move back from the fulcrum as far as you can (don't be afraid) and encourage the environment to move toward you. The balance is there. It's only a matter of finding it. And reverse the process if you find yourself too heavy for the environment.

Begin slowly but begin where you find yourself. Build it up. It gets easier. I had buckets of sand kicked in my face for years before I put myself into my own life and began to change things. Like a stuck window shade, it's a little difficult to get it started but once you do, it builds its own momentum and flies toward the ceiling.

If you're not sufficiently self-assertive, begin by asking people for things which are very slightly out of the ordinary, to get the feel of it (a waiter for the time, etc.). Don't demand; ask ("May I? . . ." "Do you have? . . ." "Would it be possible? . . ."). If you're too self-assertive, begin to pull in your horns. Ask for less and less from others that is out of their normal course.

With much kindness and respect for yourself, you will be striking a more harmonious balance with your environment and allowing the full range and textures of overtones and undertones previously blocked out to enrich your life.

39 Freedom Now!

The concept of human rights and freedoms has been attracting growing attention in the news media. The Foreign Aid Subcommittee of the Senate Foreign Relations Committee has been told by State Department officials that "the promotion of human rights around the world is a vital and integral part of United States foreign policy" and that "the United States is concerned not only with officially sanctioned murders, tortures and detentions without trial but also with political rights and civil protections." The United States cannot "stand on a street corner alone shaking our tambourine for human rights but must provide leadership for other countries."

Public pronouncements, "quiet diplomacy," "friendly persuasion" and other means of promoting these objectives are long overdue. There is, however, another kind of freedom which, not governments, but the individual people affected, needlessly deny themselves. These unfree people lose out on the riches of this birthright of freedom because of two basic errors in style: the failure to concentrate themselves in the absolute present (where they are) and a failure to discover, value, and trust their own individual identities, their own original natures (who they are).

Some are waiting for better circumstances, little realizing that good circumstances and bad circumstances are only circumstances. The so-called "breaks" do not determine the person. It is he who determines how he lives through the "breaks." Others may hug the past or hunger for the future while they close their minds to the present. Still others live thin, attenuated, unfulfilled lives because of a failure of will or nerve. They settle for less than a full portion because it's easier. Or they do not permit themselves to enter into the equations of their own lives. They jettison their individual identities to follow somebody who leads them or to imitate examples held up to them from Madison Avenue or Hollywood. Some are "sacrificing" themselves for the imagined good of another. Still others consider themselves simply "unlucky" or think they are invisibly branded inferior and "destined" for failure and unhappiness. Their pasts determine their futures. They were dealt a bad hand and they seek pity for themselves and condemnation for the phantom dealer.

What can be done for those who have abdicated the

living of their lives on one pretext or another? Must they continue to pay tribute to some self-imposed toll collector, becoming old and sullen and embittered in the process? Must they remain ill-equipped for living? How can they gain their freedom now?

Freedom now requires decisions now. First we must decide where we are. Interestingly, this is often the first thought one has on regaining consciousness. "Where am I?" Whatever your physical location happens to be, you are in the temporal present, the now. And this is where your being should be concentrated. We look beyond or behind only when we feel cheated or short-changed in the present. If you are reading these words and stop to think about what you intend to do tomorrow or should have done yesterday, you are not concentrating yourself in the present. Dwelling in the past is a way of trying to make a bargain with life to be allowed to keep what you have in exchange for not wanting more. Spending too much thought on the future cuts you off from all that is alive and possible now and leaves you unfit to handle the future when it actually does arrive. It is thus you dis—integrate. You split yourself off, away from the present, from life. You dilute yourself. You cannot be wholehearted. Experience is dimmed. You are disengaged from a living situation and your life becomes less real.

But freedom now does not consist in acting as if each fleeting moment were going to be the last. This is the false kind of freedom of the irresponsible. The truly free person is true to his whole self, his complete being, and he knows this includes the world, for he is an individual member of the world. For him to act otherwise would be impossible, disharmonious. It would be using the right hand to cut off the left hand.

Once we permit ourselves to see into the nature of our own being, we are able to become directly and immediately involved with life. We unshackle our creative energies and allow their free, natural play or expression. The person who has seen into the nature of his own being may rely on his own being—himself. He has nothing to fear. He is completely at home in the world. This cannot be achieved by memorizing old formulations or mouthing learned doctrines or expounding theories or hypotheses. It must be lived through personally. It is guided only by one's inmost being living through it. Once this quest has been accomplished, the life of the individual takes on a reality, an authenticity, an enrichment. He no longer merely acts out the motions of a meaningless existence, directed by others who are similarly acting and equally unenlightened, unfree. He no longer seeks to imitate others, to appropriate their selfness for himself, or more correctly, for the self he formerly found lacking. He is simply being; being himself, being alive, in life. He is no longer watching himself living and feeling guilty and ashamed at what he sees. His is the innocence of just being fully alive without the life-diminishing need to be his own biographer.

As a person enters into a creative relationship with life, he also automatically avoids the uncreative. He does not get involved with all that is second hand, not made his own by direct application, by using it, by living with it. All that is not truly his own, in this sense, is stripped off and discarded. This may include some elements which might have been of some value had they been "properly" or "creatively" appropriated. The fact that these elements are discarded does not mean they are bad in themselves. It means simply they are not properly one's own.

By thus returning to what is his own, irreducible self,

the individual is left with what is undeniably his, that which nobody can take from him: namely his own identity, his self, his being. As he interacts with life from the bedrock of what is completely and totally his own, he is able to enter into living situations without posing, according to his real nature, the precious nature of his own being. He is thus freed of all the false elements, the wholesale merchandise, the hand-me-downs he and others had been so ready to fasten onto him. He is freed to face life, to participate in his own being, creatively and wholeheartedly. And he is free to take the chances life offers, to exercise options, to put himself into situations without knowing the outcome in advance. It is only by being free to go into tunnels without seeking reassuring light at the other end each time that we are free to put ourselves on the line, free to let go, and live.

40 Observations

As Yogi Berra is reported to have said, "Sometimes you can observe a lot just by watching." I like to think observation is one of my specialities. I have developed these powers to the point I can invariably tell the difference between any two things without necessarily knowing what either is. That may not sound like much but if you can do that and you develop a taste for the better of the two entities, you soon create a momentum toward quality. Many of my observations are indigenous to the particular place in which I spend most of my time and would therefore not be particularly useful to a broader readership. However, a few observations might be generally helpful and may properly be included here.

I've noticed that anybody may order kosher food on a meal flight and thereby avoid the typically undistinguished food served in the coach or tourist section. By simply requesting kosher or other special food in advance (or asking your travel agent to do so) you will have the decided advantage of this specially prepared and catered food. It won't be a cordon bleu meal but it should be preferred by most passengers, and it can provide a useful conversation piece if you want one.

Have you ever tried to get the out-of-town address of somebody who has a listed telephone number? The typical response from a long distance directory-assistance operator is "I'm sorry. We're not permitted to give out that information." It's obvious they wouldn't have to omit the dividend on the stock if they accommodated you but they nevertheless regularly play the same frustrating card.

By trying a few combinations in my down time, I've figured out a simple, effective way to get this information. So far, it has worked every time. I make a collect station call to the business office of the telephone company in the city in which I want to find an address. The company routinely puts these calls through as they don't have to pay for these calls. When I'm connected, I ask for a supervisor. I explain I don't have the local directory and don't want the company to go to the trouble and expense of delivering it but that I'm trying to find the address of a subscriber who has a listed telephone and it has been suggested I get it this way. In a few seconds, the information is imparted.

Here's a ploy that can advance your career. I used to work for a large corporation whose chairman enjoyed the game of tennis. When the company moved its headquarters to a 40-story office building, I noticed a remarkable number of middle and upper management people carrying tennis gear with them when they entered and left the building. The company's elevators became filled with a rising tide of tennis enthusiasts throughout the year. While it is true that tennis became more popular during this period, I like to think that if the chairman had been an avid skier or golfer or stamp collector this would have been reflected in the corporate corridors.

The use of the company elevator as a kind of moving theater of personnel in which to gain exposure for the purpose of creating and enhancing upward mobility is not taught in any of the graduate business schools yet, but its utility is obvious. Where else can such exposure to those who can effect job transfers for you be gained? In the brief half minute or so (depending upon the number of stops) it takes the elevator to reach your departure point, an image or message can certainly be conveyed. (Advertisers often pay more than $50,000 for a 30-second commercial; here is an opportunity to beam your own message to the ideal audience and cast yourself as the star with residual benefits that could last a lifetime.)

The favorable exposure you wish to create might include your community and social responsibilities, your hobbies and interests, your dedication to the job, and so on. The props for each message are usually fairly straightforward and easily obtained. They should be chosen for their conversational value and image-creation functions. Sometimes subtlety is appropriate; at other times, you may

209

choose to be more obvious. As with any other communication process, much depends on the audience and the message to be conveyed. A little care with your timing, and you're on your way.

World-championship class bores, I have noticed, often use the expression: "Well, he (or she or it) did it again!" Whether or not you ask for elucidation, it will not be long in coming. If you were considering elective surgery (or another time-consuming project), you might go ahead with it when one of these individuals begins to fill in the details. It's a safe bet they'll still be particularizing for you when you come out of the recovery room and you can simply have the call transferred to your room. These superstars of boredom are so good at their specialty they can affect animals. Formerly contented pets often become unnerved and bristle in their presence, and may fling themselves through closed windows, shards of glass embedded in their flanks, to escape their company.

If the Peter Principle were operating properly, the world would be in the hands of shoemakers. They get the job done more often than anybody else; yet they remain shoemakers. I think professional musicians rank second. If they make a mistake in a live performance (which is relatively rare, considering the great number of opportunities for error) they get on with it and take us with them to the last note.

Competent professional advice is becoming harder to find and its price is zooming out of sight even as its benefits become increasingly important. At the same time, the practice of fee splitting is rampant. If a lawyer, for example, refers you to another lawyer who handles your matter, the first lawyer receives what is called a referral fee from the second lawyer. In effect, they split the fee between them. I find this practice objectionable for two basic reasons. The second lawyer in this example would be working for me at a sharply reduced rate and his motivation might be correspondingly weakened, particularly in terms of the priority he assigns to my case. In addition, I lose much leverage in negotiating the fee, as a large portion of it is going to be paid to the first lawyer. By thus paying two lawyers for the work of one, I am paying top dollar; at the same time I am likely to be receiving less than I would have had I gone to the second lawyer without the first lawyer's referral.

One solution to this widespread problem is simply to ask a competent practitioner in one profession to recommend a competent practitioner in another. I have discovered that competent professionals can do this very well. I might ask a lawyer whose work is excellent to recommend a good doctor, or a competent doctor to recommend a good accountant. As such referrals are given as professional courtesies and don't ordinarily involve fee splitting, I am in a position to hire the services of a competent professional, negotiate the cost, and get a high quality service.

Banks and insurance companies have received a great deal of criticism in recent years and it does seem apparent they are inheriting the earth. I have solved the problem of bank charges and the other expenses associated with checking accounts in the following way. I have two checking accounts. Neither requires any minimum balance; neither charges any monthly or per check fees. Both pay interest; both pay all the costs of banking by mail; each works slightly differently. The account at Citizens Bank and Trust Company (Park Ridge, Illinois 60666) is a United Security Account. The highest interest rate allowed by law is computed on a daily basis from the day of deposit and credited semi-annually in June and December.

After you have been a depositor long enough you will receive immediate credit on deposited checks up to a total of $500 on any given deposit date. Checks the bank recognize are routinely given immediate credit. The only drawback is that amounts drawn against your account must be redeposited by the fifteenth of the following month or a charge of one-half of one percent is levied against your account. However, if you are depositing salary checks on a regular basis this shouldn't be a problem.

The NOW (Negotiable Orders of Withdrawal) account of the Coolidge Bank and Trust Company (Watertown, Massachusetts 02072), pays 5 percent compounded and credited monthly on all deposits which have cleared. By using one or both of these accounts it is possible not only to get interest on your checking accounts and not be charged any fees but to continue to receive interest until your checks have actually arrived at the bank. And if you wish, you may pay bills in such a way as to maximize your interest.

Billions of hours are wasted each year by pedestrians waiting for traffic lights to turn green. To cut down on this waiting time and arrive at your destination in the most efficient way, the principle to follow is simple. Assuming there is no compelling reason for not taking the most direct route, such as sunniness or shade or the relative safety or attractiveness of the streets involved, the idea is to walk in the direction which will equalize the numbers of blocks in each direction which remain to be traversed if you may do so without waiting for a traffic light. For example, if your destination were five blocks east and nine blocks south, you would begin by walking south. At each corner, you would choose to walk south if the light were favorable, until you had evened the number of blocks to be walked in each direction. Thus, you would not wait for any unnecessary lights and would cover more distance in less time.

The point of these observations is that a little imagination and ingenuity can make life more rewarding and more fun. I would very much welcome any observations readers may have. Ants are marvelous creatures but they are programmed to follow certain chemical traces of their leaders to such an extent that if the latter were to move in a circular direction, they would follow unto death. Human beings can be a lot more marvelous than that!

41 The Untouchables

Like most people, I spent the first 20 or more years of my life learning the rules society teaches us in so many ways, only to find they'd been changed by the time I became an adult. During the following decade, I repeatedly collided with my environment, trying to get my life back into synchronization with the rules, but I was always a step or two out of phase. After I'd had more than my quota of figurative sand kicked into my face by a growing number of malefactors, I began to develop methods and techniques for besting a variety of wrongdoers and wresting from them what was rightfully mine, and perhaps an additional exaction for my time and trouble and for its deterrent effect. I became quite adept at redressing grievances and, in a proper case, was not loath to go up against a villainous cast, from cab drivers to conglomerates. Although I became engaged only when I was morally certain I was in the right, my docket was rarely clear. Wrongdoers, it seemed, were never in short supply.

After I'd mastered the various cures, I began to develop a systematic approach to prevention that became equally effective. But there were still certain types of miscreants who were somehow slipping through the net or between the cracks. There were, I discovered, some people with whom it was simply impossible to break even. They could damage you without recourse.

For example, if you hire the services of a lawyer and he does virtually nothing by way of handling your legal matter, you will ordinarily discover the full dimensions of his nonfeasance only after the passage of a great deal of time. Should you then disengage his services, even if you don't pay him anything for the little or nothing he's done (which is rare) you are out of position simply by virtue of all the time which has run against you without expeditious handling of your matter. You are also without a convenient remedy for this wrong. You will rarely get any satisfaction by complaining to the local bar association and, in any event, there is no way to turn back the clock.

If there were some means of identifying such people and treating them as untouchables, that is, avoiding social and commercial intercourse with them, we could add this protective shield to our wide assortment of preventives and cures. Fortunately, and despite myriad individual differences (to which our cap is doffed, our glass raised), we can observe a number of generalizations about untouchables and begin a system of classification.

High on our list of untouchables are procrastinators, such as the lawyer referred to earlier. They are generally the product of one or more overcoercing parents, I have learned. All too often, parents make excessive demands on their children and continually hector and harangue them about complying with an extensive schedule of largely inessential requirements. The resulting syndrome, in addition to procrastination, typically includes impulse buying, often of items the untouchable cannot afford, and sexual promiscuity.

I once hired a lawyer I had known at college but hadn't seen in more than twenty years, except for one or two chance encounters. In my first visit to his office, he told me about an extramarital affair he was having and pointed out a painting on the wall behind me he had impulsively bought for an alleged $12,000. It was one of the ugliest and dullest paintings (an unusual combination, to be sure, but not necessarily artistically significant) I'd seen, and looked as if the artist had mixed in a generous quantity of Mississippi mud with his oils. Unawareness of this untouchable's disability and its potential for damaging me cost more than a year of valuable time and badly snarled an important matter that I'm still trying to have straightened out. Shortly before I fired him, after some chance reading alerted me to this poisonous, and highly contaminating, condition, I asked him whether his parents had been particularly coercive, which he confirmed.

Procrastinators are extremely poor business risks and usually notch a series of heartbreaking, frustrating personal relationships. They thrive on rancor and recrimination, which reinforces their disability. Their marriages, almost invariably stormy, usually end in divorce. They spend disproportionate time and energy averting lawsuits and

216

other threats and run up much billable legal time but they are notoriously bad payers. They are often highly intelligent, glib, articulate, seductively charming, shifty, and extremely dangerous. The best way to handle them is to have no contact with them, as the only position in which you won't have a loss with this type of untouchable is the starting line.

Another frustrating untouchable is the withholder. Although these individuals make excellent treasurers, storers of goods, archivists, collectors, and the like, they are not distinguished by their generosity. Worse, if you deal with them, you are in for a series of logjams and bottlenecks. They stop the flow of ideas and material, clotting everything they touch and finally destroying all creativity, communication, and enthusiasm, like a fatal thrombosis.

Anything they borrow is on permanent loan; they seize upon all that comes into their ken, fastening it within their grasp and removing it from circulation. A prosecutor or plaintiff should be delighted to have them on the jury or the bench, but they are otherwise congestive and inefficient to work with. They also tend to be untidy as pack rats and this is a valuable clue to their identity. They suffer from constipation and other digestive disorders and may give their identities away by the constant supply of laxatives and antacids to be found in their refrigerators, cupboards, and medicine cabinets.

Perhaps the most numerically significant untouchables are those afflicted with unilateral sensitivity. They have the uncanny ability to stand on your toe without realizing it, but can pick up vibrations that would stymie a Masai teenager when something that interests them is at stake. Selfish and self-protective, they will always take more than they give.

217

They are born storytellers and excel at ridicule and defamation. They are also ruthless users and will squeeze a cooperating victim like a citrus fruit. They are shameless distorters and will never tell a story straight if coloring and twisting it will improve their position. They have no sense of propriety and their taste is poor. They are the life of the party but they are always on (and on and on). All is subjective to them and they are the subject, ready, willing, and able at all times to talk about themselves endlessly.

They tend to be pious and hypocritical. They are also extremely defensive and insecure and are perpetually taking polls so they can line up with the majority. Immature and irresponsible, apart from their inexhaustible supply of gossip and anecdotes, which may sometimes be amusing, they have nothing to offer, nor is it likely they ever will, for this untouchable, although occasionally talented, invariably lacks substance and integrity and character.

Another interesting untouchable is the individual who approaches life with only the grossest of scales. He can distinguish a sugar cube from a rhinoceros but lesser differences and distinctions appear to elude him. Black and white appear only as shades of gray and he is color-confused about the rainbow's spectrum.

This imprecise untouchable is scornful of science and mathematics and specificity generally. He is often heard to exclaim: "It's the same thing!" when comparing two entities that are different, the less desirable of which nets him a profit if he can fob it off on you. Half-truths, inaccuracies, misstatements and excuses are his stock-in-trade. His occupation often has something to do with hoopla where such an approach is, alas, still deemed useful. If pressed with a specific question, this untouchable's typical response is not the answer but an inquiry as to the questioner's standing to ask, and he will not reduce any of his puffery or promises to writing. Like cold canvassing, his approach to life is based on percentages and his loyalties may be expected to oscillate like a precious-metal detector, as they work on the same principle. It is when this particular untouchable tries to sell you something, whether tangible or intangible, that he will reveal himself most clearly. This is the time to be vigilant.

This work on untouchables is not meant to be taken as exhaustive. It is only a beginning. However, the list will not be unduly long, for as future research isolates new candidates, our system of preventives and cures will be further refined and improved so as to permit the deletion of some of these troublesome types from their places on the roster. At the present time these people are incorrigible and have had a lifetime of reinforcement to add to their early bad conditioning. In the current state of the art, I strongly recommend that initial contact with this group be avoided, while research goes on to find some relief for those desperate unfortunates who are already inextricably enmeshed with these benighted people by ties of blood and marriage and commerce.

42 Wrapping

Joseph Wood Krutch observed, "We have been deluded by the fact that the methods employed for the study of man have been, for the most part, those originally devised for the study of machines or the study of rats, and are capable, therefore, of detecting and measuring only those characteristics which the three do have in common." This work, whatever may be its faults, has avoided the delusive approach of which Mr. Krutch remarks. We have dealt exclusively with human actions, the way real people treat one another in real situations. And the unwavering focus of our attention has been on solutions instead of problems. Those proposed may have been sometimes bold, occasionally outrageous, but always effective and capable of yielding the desired result without the necessity of special training or expertise.

But no matter how effective, it would be a fundamental mistake to rely upon anybody's proposed solutions. The creative approach to life seeks the concrete beyond intellectualization, beyond abstraction. It deals with actual facts, not theoretical verbalizations; realities themselves, not statements about reality. The truth is not gained by memorizing old formulations or doctrines or theories. It is not something we know; it is something we are; it is part of us. And when we are able to become directly involved in our own lives, we take on our own identities and our lives become real, enriched, authentic. We no longer act out the motions of a meaningless existence, directed by others (who are similarly acting). We are free to be ourselves, the truest freedom of all.

The overwhelming majority of people are engaged in a neverending struggle, forced to play "catch-up ball" with their lives, always trying to come from behind with a late rally and never quite making it. Others, a very few, know the satisfactions of the free-stroking front-runner. One of America's great milers, Glenn Cunningham, when asked how he won races, is reported to have replied, "I get in the lead and stay there." This marvelous and courageous athlete had been so badly burned in a schoolhouse fire when he was eight, doctors said he would never walk. Determined not to be defeated, he became the world record-holder for the mile. It is this active approach to life which is the core and basis of *How to Get the Upper Hand*. In putting ourselves into the equations of our own lives, we change the equations and achieve results otherwise impossible. The great Antoine de Saint-Exupéry puts it this way, "Truth is not what we discover, but what we create."

At age seven, I had a rare disease. Specialists were flown in and I heard them tell my parents I would die or go blind. I don't know how most children that age would have reacted but I never believed that statement for an instant. It never became part of me. Seventeen days later, I was back at school and soon thereafter winning races. I didn't set the record for the mile but I had a pretty good kick, and I'm still kicking.

Twelve years ago, in a routine physical examination, a doctor discovered a node growing out of the side of my thyroid. I began to consult with a number of doctors. Interestingly, all of the surgeons estimated the size of the node on the high side and they all recommended surgery. The other doctors had a variety of opinions. I spent a great deal of time in the best medical library in the city in which I lived, about 90 percent of which was open to the public.

I had a thyroid scan and uptake, both of which appeared normal to the specialist who did the test (and to me). For one year I took two grains of thyroid hormone daily in order to determine what effect, if any, this would have on the node. At the end of that period I had another scan and uptake and I asked the specialist for his opinion.

"It's in the normal range," he replied. "Put your shirt on."

I disagreed with this doctor, who had specialized in thyroid therapy for more than thirty years.

"I think there are minor changes in the scan, which you can see more easily if you compare both scans side by side and the uptake is on the low side. I think surgery is indicated."

I thought he would remind me I was the patient, not the doctor, but he said nothing and retired to his study. He compared both scans carefully. There was a long silence, which he finally broke.

"I agree with you," he said quietly.

I selected a man I considered the best surgeon in the area for this condition and had the operation. The doctors, for reasons I never accepted, chose to tell me the condition was benign. However, I realized from the medication, I'd had thyroid cancer and wrote to the surgeon, explaining why I thought I'd been misinformed. I told him the only way the doubt could be resolved was to obtain the hospital record, which I was in process of doing. He replied by telling me the truth and the hospital records subsequently confirmed the malignancy. Thyroid cancer is not a particularly deadly form of the disease but if I hadn't put myself into the equation and done the homework it might have metastasized and those doctors who said I'd go blind or die might have been right at last.

Experts often make errors. In this century, Webster's Unabridged Dictionary defined "uranium" as "a worthless white metal, not found in the U.S." It would have been more accurate to have been less arrogant. We must stop falling into the error of relying on experts. We must take responsibility for our own lives. We must exercise choices. In the words of Kazantzakis, "We must knock against our destiny and knock again, until the door is opened and we save ourselves."

A healthy skepticism for the weighty pronouncements of experts is long overdue, for we have been taught to deny and doubt ourselves from birth. Entire industries have evolved that manufacture clay idols for us to worship, and fabricate new flags of a bewildering variety for us to salute.

Others deliberately commit distortions to paper, secure in the knowledge cold type will lend substance to nonsense. We buy rabbits' feet and close our eyes to the light. We are taught to covet the false and reject the real. We have been encouraged to believe in almost anything but ourselves. In fact, scientists have postulated a new form of disease which carries self-denial to new heights: an allergy to *ourself*. According to this theory, the body reacts to its own cells as if they were invaders from outside and attacks them.

The approach offered in these pages is based upon the feelings of individuals and how best and most efficiently these feelings can be ventilated to produce constructive changes. In our social, business, and professional lives, we interact with dozens of people every week. As buyers, sellers, pedestrians, passengers, invitees, guests, hosts, neighbors, friends, relatives, employees, spouses, parents, children, siblings, clients, patients, prospective clients, spectators (the list is almost endless), we are increasingly aware of a number of dissatisfactions. The press and scale of business, the speed and quantity of communications, automation, computerization, all impinge on us with numbing effects. We are becoming unpaid guinea pigs, involuntarily conscripted by a society hell-bent on obtaining our approval even as it turns us upside down in order to shake loose the last few coins in our pockets. The junk telephone call has become a reality. There now exists an automated dialing system that can place as many as a thousand calls per day of a prerecorded sales message and can record the responses of each prospect contacted before hanging up and dialing another number. A major food company has a food ready for us that will prevent digestion, as well as foods impossible to digest; it hopes to market those by 1979.

How we feel must be given expression if we are to be in

good health. Repressing our feelings produces a host of psychogenic illnesses. Suppression of feelings narrows the lines of communication and leads to alienation and a loss of desirable human interaction. This unchanneled energy is left to collect until it explodes with uncontrollable force to damage and destroy situations and relationships, sometimes life itself.

The way to take control of our lives is to exercise choices. The methods and techniques set forth in these pages are effective and have already been used to advantage by a number of people. They require no special training, knowledge, or expertise and they are completely independent of one another. Only those deemed useful need be employed. But beyond this or that method or technique lies the fundamental attitude that changes can be effected by an individual, that improvements can be made by a single person, that one person can make a difference. And this is a fact that bears restating. Alert and resourceful individuals can create new ways of achieving desired results in their lives.

Such an approach has become a necessary alternative to an unrewarding life, for there is no longer the opportunity for graceful retreat. A Thoreau might enjoy his splendid solitude at Walden Pond but such oases have all but disappeared. Land developers and a population committed to the internal combustion engine have brought television, telephones, and trash to the wilderness. Even the long-suffering Smokey the Bear finally succumbed to the incivilities of civilization.

There is another, much more dangerous retirement from life that should be mentioned. We often hear people make statements which attempt to make a verbal pact with life, a kind of Faustian bargain. The statements usually begin with the word "if." A common example is "If I could live to be 70 (or some other finite number) and be in good health, I'd be satisfied." The main reason I think this sort of statement is dangerous is that I am convinced it weakens the speaker's grip on life and programs and conditions the speaker for his or her demise. Such statements program a goal stated as a product instead of as a process. In so doing, the speaker is relating the attaining of a goal to a relinquishing of something valuable. This is a very bad bargain for it gives away something for nothing. In the example given, if good health is desired, the speaker should try to achieve good health without being prepared to give up his or her life for it in this unreal way.

Finally, it must be clear that getting the upper hand is not to be done at any price and without regard to the consequences. It is not intended to be used to take unfair advantage of people and situations. It is not designed as another form of ruthlessness and brutality and it is never intended as a means of attack. There will be many occasions when compassion and forbearance properly take precedence, when no action will be taken or perhaps a gentle word is spoken by way of reply to a particular breach of decorum. We must allow others room for play and experimentation and miscalculation even as we ourselves may be allowed the same prerogatives. But when it is apparent the other side has no wish to listen to reason and intends to disregard our interests and continue to exact unacceptable tolls, the methods and techniques set forth in these pages will provide a convenient and useful beginning on which to build effective responses in controlling such unprovoked and damaging actions. The intent of this book is to furnish a range of easily applied methods and techniques for limiting or eliminating the abuses of power with which we may occasionally be confronted. But it is absolutely essential that this be done without ourselves joining the ranks of those who abuse their power. By achieving the desired results in our encounters with such people, *we will begin to think differently about ourselves* and this self-confidence and self-respect will help deter encroachments. By quickly and effectively countering these formerly expensive and humiliating situations, we free ourselves. Our lives become more integrated and unified and we are free to chart a sensible route in the direction we wish to take with our lives. Like great sculptors, we thus chip away the meaningless and unnecessary until nothing stands between ourselves and our goals. And it is never too late to begin.